Local Food, Local Restaurants, Local Recipes

The MINNESOTA HOMEGROWN COOKBOOK

Presented by Renewing the Countryside

FOREWORD BY GARRISON KEILLOR

Voyageur Press

For our friend, mentor, and unbeatable
dinner companion, Dick Broeker

First published in 2008 by Voyageur Press, an imprint of Quarto Publishing Group USA Inc., 400 First Avenue North, Suite 400, Minneapolis, MN 55401. This second edition published in 2014.

The information in this book is true and complete to the best of our knowledge. All recommendations are made without any guarantee on the part of the author or Publisher, who also disclaim any liability incurred in connection with the use of this data or specific details.

We recognize, further, that some words, model names, and designations mentioned herein are the property of the trademark holder. We use them for identification purposes only. This is not an official publication.

Voyageur Press titles are also available at discounts in bulk quantity for industrial or sales-promotional use. For details write to Special Sales Manager at Quarto Publishing Group USA Inc., 400 First Avenue North, Suite 400, Minneapolis, MN 55401.

To find out more about our books, join us online at www.voyageurpress.com.

Voyageur Press Editor: Michael Dregni
Project Managers: Elizabeth Noll and Caitlin Fultz

A Renewing the Countryside Project
2637 27th Avenue South, Suite 17
Minneapolis, MN 55404
www.renewingthecountryside.org

Support for this project provided through a grant from North Central Region Sustainable Agriculture Research and Education.
Project Director: Jan Joannides
Creative Director: Brett Olson
Editors: Alice Tanghe, Jan Joannides, and Stephanie Larson
Writers: Tim King and Alice Tanghe
Additional Writing: Elijah Goodwell, Grace Brogan, and Arlene Jones
Recipe Editors: Alice Tanghe and Mary Broeker
Senior Photographer: Anthony Brett Schreck
Photographers: Brett Olson, Kristi Link Fernholz, John Connelly, Richard Hamilton Smith, and Dave Holman
Advisory Committee: Mary Broeker, Jan Joannides, Tim King, Chuck Knierim, Brett Olson, and Alice Tanghe
Project Assistants: Beth Munnich, Andi McDaniel, Derric Pennington, Margaret Schnieders, and Sarah Johnson

Library of Congress Control Number: 2014944251

Printed in China

CONTENTS

FOREWORD

BY GARRISON KEILLOR

I grew up a few steps from a half-acre vegetable garden, and it pretty much ruined me for fine dining forever after. When you've eaten sweet corn ten minutes removed from the stalk, you've experienced intense sensual pleasure at a young age, and what can the great chefs of New York and Paris offer to compete with it?

My father John loved sweet corn and most other fresh vegetables, also raspberries and strawberries, and after Christmas he pored over the seed catalogues with all the varieties with names like race horses: Contender, Kentucky Wonder, Little Marvel, Early Perfection, Silver Queen, Early Prolific, and I recall a broccoli called the Brigadier. And also Detroit Supreme Beets. He was a Minnesota farm boy, and even after we moved to the outskirts of Minneapolis, he preferred to butcher his own chickens rather than buy the plastic-wrapped stuff at Super Valu. In the spring, he plowed the half acre and planted the rows—the strawberry beds and raspberry patch lay to the east so he planted melons and cucumbers on the west side of the plot, a regiment of corn to the rear, the pole beans and tomatoes and peas and root crops in the middle—and as we ate the last Mason jars of Mother's canned goods from the shelves in the laundry room and cleaned out the freezer, we awaited the glories of July and August and September.

In sweet corn season, Mother fixed Sunday dinner or weekday supper, got the pot roast or meatloaf or hot dish all set, and had a big pot of water boiling on the stove before we kids were dispatched to pick the corn. We picked an armload and started husking it as we walked to the house and put the naked ears in the boiling water for a few minutes, the prayer was said, the platter of steaming corn on the cob was brought to the table, we distributed it with tongs and slathered it with butter and salted it and ate it in our hands, chewing the kernels off either in lateral or circular fashion, and we never ever said, "This sure is good sweet corn!" Never. You'd only say that if somebody served you week-old storebought corn, to make them feel better. The ten-minute corn was beyond goodness—it was a spiritual experience, proof that God exists and that He loves you, and there is no need to compliment God on the sweet corn, what's necessary is to love this gift and enjoy it, and we did.

There were six of us children, so labor was cheap, and the soil was good black loam, and the output of that half-acre was just prodigious. Awesome, in fact. The gross yield of forty tomato plants can give you daily salads, bushels of tomatoes to stew and can, and bags of tomatoes to take to relatives in the city. But the greatest prize is for the boy hoeing the tomatoes

who reaches down and rescues one and wipes the dust off and bites into it. That is pure pleasure, a privilege offered to few, and after it, you will never be happy with any tomato you buy in a store. You hold it to your nose and there is no tomatoness there whatsoever. It was bred for shelf life and strip-mined in Mexico, or the Imperial Valley of California, and artificially ripened, and now it has no more tomato essence than your shoe. This is why vinaigrette dressing was invented: to provide some flavor for denatured vegetables.

Where I grew up in the late forties and fifties, in Brooklyn Park township along the Mississippi five miles north of the Minneapolis city limits, there were truck farms—"truck" here means "miscellany," not the motorized vehicle—that raised vegetables for sale at the farmers market near downtown. There was a farm that specialized in radishes and onions and another that mostly raised strawberries. The Fishers had a big asparagus operation, and Fred Peterson raised sweet corn and peas, and there were potato farms north of us along the West River Road and over towards Osseo. A boy could hop on his bike and ride off any summer morning and find work there, put in eight hours picking potatoes and earn fifty cents an hour plus a bag of unsellable scabby potatoes to take home for supper.

My family was in the first wave of settlement after World War II. My dad got a G.I. loan to buy lumber, and he built the house himself on an acre of cornfield he bought from Fred Peterson, and other houses sprang up near us, and all of them had big vegetable gardens. That was the beauty of the acre lot: you put a house and yard on half of it and farmed the other half. When the value of land zoomed in the late sixties, people sold off that back half-acre. It was ironical—the urge to have some land on which to raise a garden led to a land rush that wiped out the gardens—and soon the lovers of sweet corn and tomatoes had to settle far from the city and endure long commutes.

And most of us children who grew up on fresh tomatoes went off to live lives that did not include a garden. All but one of my father's siblings—Lawrence, Jim, Eleanor, Elizabeth, Bob, Josephine—had vegetable gardens of considerable breadth and variety, and none of my five siblings raise their own food and neither do I. We all became city dwellers and had better things to do with our time. We went to the movies. We stayed late at the office. We dashed from home to a meeting and then back to the office and en route, hungry, we saw the golden arches and drove up to the intercom and got the burger and fries and ate it as we drove. There was no McTomato or McCorn on the menu.

The co-op movement of the seventies placed a premium on Local and Organic, and that has led us back toward the garden. In my neighborhood co-op I can occasionally find tomatoes that smell of tomato, and if I drive over to Wisconsin in the summer I will eventually find a pickup truck parked by a field and a big sign SWEET CORN and a boy sitting in the shade. And if my wife and I go to the right restaurant, we will find a menu that tells where the salad comes from and where the fish was caught and who raised the cow who provided the strip steak, which is always of interest.

I can never be a boy again standing barefoot in a garden on a sunny day and holding a ripe tomato in my hand—don't really want to be him anyway—but this lovely book gives me hope that something beautiful that I thought had passed away has actually come full circle and that other people in Minnesota share this same longing for fresh food. Back in my childhood, the Sunday paper sometimes ran stories about What the World Will Be Like In the Year 2000 and, in addition to travel by rocket cars and living in glass-domed houses, the futurists agreed that people in 2000 would take their meals in the form of pills. This did not strike us as something to look forward to. The futurists were thinking only of convenience—we are a restless people and notoriously impatient and so you might assume that we'd prefer to have dinner in the form of capsules, gulp them down, save ourselves the trouble—but in fact we have a secret longing for pleasure, too. We are some of the hardest-working people on the planet, and we deserve a little reward now and then. A fresh tomato, sliced, with chilled cucumber and pepper and onion. An ear of corn. Six small red potatoes, boiled in their skins. All of it homegrown. From this, one can regain faith in divine providence and restore a sense of the kindness and beauty of the world and resolve to rise up tomorrow and try to do what needs to be done.

INTRODUCTION

All food is not created equal. Anyone who bites into a just-picked tomato on a warm summer day knows that it hardly resembles that tomato-like thing you get in Minnesota grocery stores in January. And cheese crafted by an artisan cheesemaker is worlds apart from those single-wrapped, processed slices that many of us grew up on.

This is a book about homegrown food. Not necessarily homegrown, as in your own garden, but homegrown by farmers and producers across the state.

In this book we take you on a journey. It begins on the North Shore and traverses the state, covering the Red River Valley, Minnesota River Valley, Pine and Lakes Country, Bluff Country, and the Twin Cities. It delves into the interdependent relationships between farmers and chefs, between local ingredients and good food.

We share the stories of chefs and cooks who are passionate about local foods. They know that food raised by local farmers is fresher and tastes better than food that travels across the country—or the world. They willingly adjust their menus to incorporate the freshest local ingredients. Seasonality is something they embrace.

The farmers we visit are equally as passionate about the food they produce. They use innovative and sustainable techniques to raise the best food and raise it in a way that cares for the environment. They are concerned about treating their animals humanely and about delivering a product that is healthy for those who eat it.

In addition to farmers, we visit food gatherers who skillfully tap maple trees, fish Lake Superior, or harvest wild rice. We also meet artisan foodmakers who create a mouthwatering array of cheeses, wines, jams, and other tasty morsels.

Tucked among the stories are an array of tantalizing recipes from the chefs and cooks featured. They demonstrate what can be created from the fresh, seasonal food we have locally.

As you make your way through the stories and recipes, you may not even notice that there are no bay scallops or basmati rice recipes. Oh sure, you'll find recipes with chocolate and lemons, but you'll also be surprised by the rich and amazingly diverse palate showcased here, from corn chowder to morel mushroom, goat cheese, and asparagus fettuccine.

The chefs and farmers featured here are just a fraction of the growing number who are changing the way we think about food. We're in the midst of a local foods revolution. It tastes better. It's healthier. And it's better for the planet.

We don't suggest you give up oranges, coffee, or chocolate, but protest a little when someone tries to sell you an apple from New Zealand in October. French and California wines are great, but try one of the new Minnesota wines. Plant a tomato, visit a farmers' market, join a CSA or a food co-op. Ask your favorite grocery store, restaurant, local hospital, or your child's school if they buy locally grown food. If they don't, encourage them to do so. This isn't about being fanatical but rather about using common sense—the sense that tells you when something tastes good and is good for you and your community.

Eat locally grown food because it is fresh. Eat locally grown food because it is healthy. Eat it because you care about supporting a sustainable, healthy countryside and because you want small farms to continue to be viable. Eat locally grown food because you can.

Enjoy!

NORTH SHORE

ANGRY TROUT CAFE

Dockside Fish Market

*T*he *Angry Trout Cafe Notebook* is dedicated to Marybeth and Martha, George Wilkes' children. The dedication reads, "May the failings of my generation lead to the awakening of yours."

George is the co-owner and co-founder of the Angry Trout Cafe in Grand Marais, along with his wife, Barb LaVigne. He wrote the book as a way to explain to Angry Trout's customers, friends, the world, and perhaps himself, his deepening and broadening thinking about sustainability and where his little cafe at the end of the pier on the edge of a big cold lake fits into a larger picture. He subtitled his book *Friends, Recipes, and the Culture of Sustainability*.

George writes, "I like to think of the success of our cafe as being dependent on the amount of meaning that our customers experience. On a basic level, good food and service at an acceptable price is the standard measure when going out to eat—but what if that delicious swordfish dinner contributes to the decline of the Atlantic swordfish population?"

Given two restaurants of equal quality, George believes customers will choose the one with the better stories. He contends, "Sustainability is a powerful story."

"What George and Barb are doing is great—and it's working," says Shele Toftey, whose family supplies the Angry Trout with fresh and smoked fish from Lake Superior. "That's what's amazing. It seems like each year they get more into it." What George and Barb

Barb LaVigne and George Wilkes

are getting into, in part, is forming strong bonds with the residents of the lakeside community of Grand Marais.

Those bonds have built understanding and trust that transcends the occasional petty differences that can arise between neighbors. Shele's had some differences with George over a few of his ideas about sustainability, but she acknowledges that everyone is welcome to his or her opinion. Besides, she values the fact that she can walk the thirty feet or so from her family's Dockside Fish Market to the Angry Trout Cafe to borrow a head of lettuce if she runs out.

Relationships that allow borrowing lettuce from your neighbor may be one thing George had in mind when he used the term "culture of sustainability" in the subtitle of his book.

For their part, George and Barb prize the fact that they can see Toftey's fishing boat coming off Lake Superior most summer mornings with the day's herring catch. They know that the fish they'll be serving their customers will be only hours old. They also know that it takes dedicated and rugged individuals to head out onto the lake at daylight to gillnet herring. Gillnetting is a fishing technique brought to the area by Scandinavian immigrants. It is an art form that requires skill and endurance in nice weather, and the weather on the big lake isn't always nice.

Then there is the excellent customer service. "Every morning I look in their cooler and I pretty much know what they go through," Shele says. "We almost always get it right, and they have fresh fish on hand. The few times they've run out, they just walk over and let us know. We can get it over there in two minutes."

The identity of the Angry Trout Cafe, along with its famous fish 'n chips and grilled Lake Superior fish of the day, is linked to the Toftey's and that, in turn, to Lake Superior's waters, people, and history. That can make for some pretty interesting fish stories. Stories like how Shele grew up on Oregon's Pacific coast and used to fish the long line boats of Alaska for halibut and black cod. Stories about how Shele met Harley in Alaska while they were fishing for salmon, and how they married and came back to an inland sea.

When the herring season on Lake Superior closes during November spawning, the Tofteys go inland to Greenwood Lake. There, for a few weeks before it ices up, they net lake herring and whitefish. Some of the whitefish served at the Angry Trout comes from the Tofteys, but that's most likely smoked. That's because when the Tofteys are netting whitefish in November, the Angry Trout is closed for the season.

The rare treat of fresh whitefish that sometimes shows up on the menu at the Angry Trout Cafe likely came from members of the Grand Portage Band of Ojibwe. They are the only commercial fishermen who can set nets for fish other than herring in Lake Superior because of their treaty rights. "If you ever see fresh whitefish on the specials board, order it right away because it won't be there very long!" George advises.

A visit to the Angry Trout spawns many questions. Who made the beautiful carving of the blue herons on the door to the cafe? Why are the organic cotton napkins so small? Where were these plates made? Who raised the delicious pork you can now find on the menu? Do they make that delicious sourdough bread right here? And why is the trout so angry?

There are some answers at hand. The answer to the last question is provided by Ms. Elaine Fisch, renowned medium to the spirit world and founder of the Society for the Prevention of Cruelty to Crystals, on page two of *The Angry Trout Cafe Notebook*. As for the sourdough bread, Toni Mason—of Grand Marais' own Good Harbor Hill Bread Company—baked it.

George and Barb are pleased to serve Toni's bread. And they're pleased a local woodworker made the chairs for the cafe and another local, Kimball Creek Woodworks, crafted the salt-shakers and pepper mills. By supporting local artisans who make products from renewable resources and farmers who grow food organically, George and Barb hope they are helping to build a better world for their daughters.

Meanwhile, Shele Toftey is wondering if her nine-year-old twins will someday be interested in fishing, or running the Dockside Fish Market. "There are so many things to get kids' attention now; you never know what will happen," she says, "but it would be wonderful if when they got older, they wanted to fish with us."

As a businesswoman, Shele is impressed with George and Barb's success. As a mother, she may be wondering if in their work lies the seed of possibility that her daughters will carry on the Toftey tradition. "We've always been fishermen," she says. "The Toftey family were fishermen in Norway before they came to Lake Superior."

For her daughters' sake, she hopes that George and Barb, as well as she and Harley, can get more things right than wrong.

Shele Toftey and a smoked herring at the Dockside Fish Market

Harley Toftey, left, fishing on Lake Superior

WILD MUSHROOM-TOMATO BISQUE

Serves 4

½ cup sliced leek
¼ cup minced shallot
1 stalk celery, chopped
1 teaspoon dried dill
2 tablespoons butter
2 cups sliced fresh shiitake mushrooms
1 16-ounce can crushed tomatoes
1½ cups vegetable stock
Salt and white pepper to taste
½ cup heavy cream
1 clove garlic, minced

½ cup additional fresh sliced mushrooms
¼ cup chopped fresh dill

Heat butter in a large pot, and sauté leek, shallot, celery, and dill for about 4 minutes. Add mushrooms and sauté until tender. Add tomatoes, stock, salt, and pepper, and bring to a boil. Reduce heat, cover, and simmer for 20 minutes.

Add cream and garlic. Using an immersion blender (or a regular blender), blend soup until smooth. Heat throughly and check seasoning.

For garnish: sauté an additional ½ cup of sliced mushrooms in butter. Place sautéed mushroom slices on top of soup with chopped fresh dill.

SMOKED HERRING WITH CRANBERRY HORSERADISH SAUCE

½ cup sour cream
¼ cup sugar
1 tablespoon horseradish
1¼ cups fresh or frozen cranberries
2 tablespoons minced red onion
Smoked herring and/or smoked, de-boned trout
Slices of French bread

In a bowl, mix sour cream, sugar, and horseradish. In a blender or food processor, blend cranberries and onion to a slightly chunky consistency. Do not liquefy. Add cranberry-onion blend to sour cream mixture and mix. Refrigerate for a while to blend the flavors.

Serve with whole smoked herring or de-boned smoked trout and slices of baguette.

BLUEBERRY CREAM TART

By Misha Martin, available at Angry Trout or at Misha Martin's Sweets

CRUST
¾ cup unsalted butter
½ cup powdered sugar
2 cups all-purpose flour

Preheat oven to 300°F. Cream the butter in a mixer bowl on medium. Turn to low, and add flour and sugar. Mix until just mixed and crumbly. Press into an 11-inch tart pan with removable bottom. Bake for 15 to 20 minutes until slightly golden. Cool on rack.

FILLING
8 ounces cream cheese, at room temperature
½ cup sour cream
½ cup powdered sugar

In mixer bowl, cream the softened cream cheese. Add sugar and sour cream, and blend on medium until smooth and fluffy. Pour into cooled tart shell and smooth top. Refrigerate.

BERRY LAYER
3 cups fresh blueberries, cleaned
1 cup sugar
1 cup water

Put berries in a strainer over a pan. Simmer sugar and water together in a saucepan for 1 minute. Take off heat and pour over berries immediately. Toss berries slightly in strainer.

Take syrup from the catch pan under the berries and pour over berries once more, with the saucepan as the catchpan. Drain berries completely and distribute over top of refrigerated filling. They will be a little sticky and hold together nicely. Refrigerate until served.

Remaining liquid can be boiled down and used as syrup with pancakes or ice cream, or can be mixed with soda water to make a blueberry soda.

CHEZ JUDE
AND WAVES OF
SUPERIOR CAFE

DragSmith Farms

Chef Judi Barsness' menus reflect the freshest offerings of the seasons. She calls her contemporary flavors "Minnisine," a portmanteau of Minnesota and cuisine, describing her commitment to regionally grown, naturally raised, or wild ingredients. On the North Shore of Lake Superior, she's quick to point out that their harvests reach beyond the land, to the northern lakes and streams, for staples such as wild rice and freshwater fish.

Judi, a second-generation chef, kindled her passion for the culinary arts in her mother's French kitchen. She studied at the Institute of America, Greystone Campus in Napa Valley, the National Baking Center with acclaimed Master Baker Didier Rasada, and with renowned chef Alice Waters at Chez Panisse. Her career in northern Minnesota began in the 1990s when she opened the Coho Cafe and Bakery for the popular Bluefin Bay Resort in Tofte. Her success led to the creation of Chez Jude in Grand Marais, which she co-founded with her husband, Peter.

The restaurant brought a fine-dining experience to the picturesque harbor town and quickly gained a local customer base. A loyal following grew, extending through Canada, Minnesota, and Wisconsin. In 2012 Judi closed Chez Jude restaurant but retained the Chez Jude name for her catering, culinary classes,

Judi Barsness

and consulting business. "It was time for us to move into the next chapter of our lives," says Judi, "to enjoy our cabin at the end of the caribou trail, spend more time with our family, each other, and traveling. Consulting, catering, and teaching cooking classes on this more personal level is so much fun."

Chez Jude Catering specializes in the increasing number of destination weddings. Drawn to the North Shore's natural beauty, her clients tend to share her care for sustainable, fresh, locally grown food. Her artful presentations of seasonal cuisine are poetic compositions, odes to the romantic setting. In the end, however, it is the flavors that win the day.

"Freshness is the key," says Judi. "When you're dealing with local suppliers, you're getting the freshest food you can possibly get. That freshness, and the sustainable manner in which the food was raised or harvested, provides an enhanced flavor . . . real food with real flavor." On another level, Judi knows that she is not only supporting local growers, but also supporting sustainability of the environment and the economy where she lives. "It's like a big circle. We all support each other. This is all very important to me as a chef, as a business person, and as a citizen of not only my community, but of my planet."

According to Judi, working where the seasons are short, the rocks are hard, and the winters are long necessitates a community of effort to overcome challenges. She partners with farmers in northern Minnesota and Wisconsin to help fill gaps in the larder that the northern climate cannot satisfy. One such partner, farmers Maurice and Gail Smith of DragSmith Farms, supplies organic produce year round. DragSmith Farms also partners with neighboring farms to distribute meat, dairy, and other farmed and foraged products.

The farm is nestled in the meandering Yellow River outside of Barron, Wisconsin, an hour and forty-five minutes northeast of Minneapolis. The 104 acres stretch along the river banks and provide a home to a variety of wildlife including eagles, deer, and bear.

"We do approximately 30 of the acres in the vegetable rotation," says Gail. But a surprising amount of the farm's business happens in her greenhouses. "I have two greenhouses, running full time, double and triple stacked with microgreens. Now we're now into our third!" Popular in contemporary cuisine as a distinctive replacement for typical salad vegetables, microgreens are the tender shoots of various edibles, including lettuces, herbs, beets, radishes, chards, and cabbages, harvested not long after sprouting, when the first leaves develop.

Maurice and Gail stumbled across microgreens during a fifteen-minute conference presentation. They had wanted a vegetable to produce year round in the greenhouse. "And it went crazy!" says Gail. "I had absolutely nobody to learn anything from, so I just learned from my own experience." Now the farm produces around thirty-five varieties of microgreens and sells them individually or in blends such as the bright, springy, fresh-tasting Mississippi Greens.

Though the Smiths manage a subscription CSA and sell to a variety of grocery stores, serving Twin Cities restaurants comprises the bulk of their business. They succeed in this challenging niche by providing excellent communication and ease of service. They communicate constantly with their chefs, sending weekly availability lists and delivery updates. Gail organizes one-on-one chef consultations throughout the year. "We meet and talk about vegetables they would like to see available; things that they would like but haven't seen locally produced." It also benefits her farm planning, she explains, "so I know whether or

Maurice and Gail Smith,
DragSmith Farms

not the restaurant is going to go through ten pounds of broccoli a week or a hundred!"

Chef Judi prizes DragSmith for the unsurpassed quality and variety of their produce, especially the spring vegetables. She likes to pair a fresh piece of fish, caught by local Harley Toftey, alongside a salad of DragSmith pea tendrils with lemon thyme vinaigrette. Judi has happily brought her relationship with the farm back to Bluefin Bay's Resorts, where she has returned as consulting executive chef.

Judi helped establish Waves of Superior Cafe, a concept paired with the destination spa at Bluefin's sister resort, Surfside. The cafe serves a wonderfully diverse menu. Breakfast includes several varieties of waffle, such as a Belgian-style with Caribou Cream Maple Syrup, from neighboring Lutsen, or heartier wild rice waffles with house-cured bacon and poached eggs. For lunch, you'll find grass-fed beef or bison burgers from Northstar Bison and farm-fresh salads with specialty greens from DragSmith Farms. The assortment includes some less typical treasures, such as a chicken bánh mì, fresh steamed mussels, and shrimp with soba noodles. A three-course afternoon tea is served daily, complete with fresh pastries, finger sandwiches, and sweets to accompany Judi's selection of organic tea and coffee.

To have a complete experience of Judi's "Minnisine," join one of her cooking classes held at the North House Folk School in Grand Marais or at the Waves of Superior Cafe, or arrange for a private class in home or cabin. Judi commences with lessons in sourcing and sustainability, often taking the students to the local co-op or fish market. Menus are seasonal and locally inspired, and instruction is hands on. Each student can expect to learn a variety of techniques and recipes for both cooking and baking. Judi allows students ample time to sit down and enjoy their work throughout the day. At the end of the class, the students dine together on their final courses, paired with Judi's selection of wine and beer.

Judi loves the energy of these intimate experiences. She is a proud emissary of culinary passion, helping her diners expand their palates, and exploring the fundamentals of cooking, baking, and the sustainable cuisines of the world—all through the lens of her "Minnisine."

With wild rice harvested from the northern waters, fresh seasonal asparagus, ramps foraged from the eponymous Onion River, and morels from the forest floor, these recipes truly represent Judi Barsness' North Shore "Minnisine." Start with a spring microgreen salad with lemon thyme vinaigrette, then serve the Wild Rice Orzotto followed by a protein of your choice, prepared with Herbes de Provence Rub.

LEMON THYME VINAIGRETTE

Yields about 2 cups

A lovely light spring and summer vinaigrette made with Meyer lemons. Serve as a wonderful complement to fresh greens or as a drizzle over fresh asparagus, haricots verts, or vegetables hot off the grill.

$1/2$ cup plus 2 tablespoons fresh-squeezed lemon juice
$1/2$ cup honey
$1^1/_4$ cups olive oil
1 heaping tablespoon fresh thyme, minced
4 shallots, minced
Salt and pepper to taste

Add lemon juice and honey to a food processor or blender. Turn on the processor and carefully drizzle olive oil steadily through tube or lid. Whisk in shallots and thyme.

WILD RICE ORZOTTO WITH ASPARAGUS, RAMPS, AND MORELS

A North Woods, North Shore, "Minnisine" delight.
Serves 8

$1^1/_2$ cups wild rice, cooked in equal parts stock and water
$2^1/_2$ cups cooked orzo, cooked in equal parts stock and water (toasted optional)
1 stick butter
$1/2$ cup sliced spring ramps, white part only
2 teaspoons minced garlic
2 cups sliced morel mushrooms
2 cups chopped asparagus
$1/2$ cup equal parts chopped parsley, rosemary, and thyme
$1/2$ cup dry white wine
$1^1/_2$ cups chicken stock or vegetable stock
$1/2$ cup cream sherry
1 cup shredded Parmesan cheese
Salt, pepper, and additional grated Parmesan cheese to taste

Melt the butter in a large, wide-bottom pan over medium heat. Sauté the ramps and garlic until soft. Add the mushrooms, asparagus, and herbs, then sauté until liquid is almost gone. Pour in the wine and reduce by half. Then add the stock and reduce until only about one tablespoon remains. Stir in the cooked rice and orzo. Add cream sherry and reduce again until only about one tablespoon remains. Stir in Parmesan cheese. Season to taste with salt and pepper. Finish with additional cheese and herb mixture if desired.

Left: Orzotto

Bluefin Bay Resort

HERBES DE PROVENCE RUB

Use for fish, meats, wild game, or poultry.

1 cup olive oil

3 tablespoons minced garlic

3 tablespoons herbs de Provence (dried mixture of thyme, rosemary, sage, lavender, basil, fennel seed, marjoram, and summer savory, available in the spice section of your local grocery)

Fresh cracked black pepper and kosher salt, to taste

Whisk all ingredients together. Rub on meats and let marinate for 2 hours prior to cooking.

WILD BLUEBERRY MAPLE CRÈME BRÛLÉE

A great dessert to serve after a hearty stew. Judi uses heavy cream from Cedar Summit, locally harvested maple syrup from Caribou Cream Maple Syrup, and blueberries that she and her forager/CSA friends harvest from their woodland properties on the North Shore, or organic berries purchased through the local Whole Foods Cooperative.

2 cups heavy cream

1/2 whole vanilla bean, scraped (or 2 teaspoons pure vanilla)

1 egg

3 large egg yolks

7 tablespoons real maple syrup

6 tablespoons small wild blueberries (fresh or frozen)

4 tablespoons turbinado sugar (raw sugar)

Four 8 oz. ramekins

Preheat oven to 325°F. Scald the heavy cream with halved and scraped vanilla bean (or use pure liquid vanilla). In mixing bowl, combine the whole egg, yolks, and maple syrup until well mixed. Temper the egg mixture by adding one third of the hot cream into the eggs while whisking constantly. Add remaining hot cream and mix. (Tempering the egg mixture prevents the eggs from turning into scrambled eggs!) Strain the mixture, removing the vanilla bean.

Place about 1 tablespoon of blueberries into the ramekins. Fill half full with the custard. Add a few additional blueberries, and fill ramekins with custard.

Set the ramekins in a baking pan; fill baking pan with boiling water halfway up the sides of the ramekins. Bake until set, approximately 40 minutes.

Remove ramekins from the water bath and let cool before covering and storing. Refrigerate 8 hours prior to serving. Can be stored up to 2 to 3 days.

Blot any moisture that is on the top of the ramekins. Sprinkle turbinado sugar or maple sugar on the custard, and caramelize with a chef's torch or under the broiler.

ELLERY HOUSE BED AND BREAKFAST

Park Lake Farm

inter is long and serene in northern Minnesota. There is time for the snow to softly accumulate. To ski. To lay another log on the fire . . . and another. To sleep in. Spring is a long way off. It may not even come this year.

In winter's grip, this would seem true to all but those few who are truly in tune. They hear the owls in January, the great grey and great horned, hooting and frolicking. They are aware of stirrings.

In February, the eelpout—the most Minnesotan of fish—migrate and mate under lifeless ice. It is then that Joel Rosen stirs. He feels it. He hears it. And in the depths of winter's already faltering clutch, Joel begins his Park Lake Farm garden near Mahtowa.

Don't despair if you can't visit Joel until early March; he'll still have time to visit. Maybe he'll share a cup of his notoriously muscular coffee, with a spot of syrup from his sugar bush. If you visit him in mid-March, you may locate him shearing sheep. He may tell you to brew your own coffee while his conversation is limited to a few scattered sentences. He may mention that he's delayed a few weeks on planting.

And, you may lean against the cold wall of the silent barn and hear the cutting of shears on thick, oily wool, hear Joel grunt as he lays the ewe down, bleating, and feel the hotness of the coffee in the back of your mouth.

Joan and Jim Halquist

Sheep shearing barely precedes maple syrup time at Park Lake Farm. There is often a story recounted that at time's beginning, maple sap, already viscous and sweet, dripped from trees. When the first people discovered this, they did what you and I would do—they lay down by the maples and drank syrup until they fell asleep. The creator came to look in on his creations, but he found the village empty and the cook fires cold. When he discovered the people lying under the maples, corpulent and soft, he stormed and raged about the sugar bush and set out to put things right. And now, as any Minnesotan who has spent time in the sugar bush can tell you, it takes about forty gallons of sap to make a gallon of syrup.

But the creator must have been distracted when he passed by Park Lake. "We have an average of about thirty gallons of sap to one gallon of syrup, and one year we were twenty to one," Joel says. "When it's twenty to one, it's half the work, half the firewood to make and stoke, and half the sap to lift." That translates to 1,200 fewer gallons of sap to haul and cook if you, like Joel has on occasion, make sixty gallons of syrup. With such a ratio, corpulence isn't far off.

"I used to think this stuff was expensive until I came out and helped Joel cook it," says Jim Halquist, who along with his wife Joan, is the owner of Duluth's Ellery House Bed and Breakfast.

Jim, who is a longtime friend and customer of Joel's, knows the truth about syrup in a way that transcends the mere telling. He's hauled the buckets, stoked the fires, and helped Joel finish a batch of syrup after it has come off Park Lake Farm's home-made sap evaporator.

"Jim and Joan buy about twenty-four quarts a year from us," Joel says. "They might like a little more, but I've only got so much. I like to make sure all my customers get some." So when the Halquists provide you with maple syrup for your Ellery House stuffed French toast, know that it is precious and rare.

Like their friend Joel, the Halquists take pleasure in providing the rarities. At their gracious breakfast table they serve good, nourishing fare and interesting conversation. When guests first enter Ellery House, they experience first the aroma, then the flavor of Joan's macadamia nut chocolate chip cookies.

Jim, a minister's son, thinks of his work as a sort of ministry as well. "My father took care of the needs of the soul," he says. "A lot of people who come here have had a physically and mentally trying week. A stay at Ellery House can soothe their tired body and mind."

A comfortable place with unpretentious elegance, Jim says, "It's a little like coming to your grandmother or great-aunt's house. It's a vision we have where keeping a house is a vocation.

It used to be an art. Nowadays, you go to Byerly's and buy the cookies or brownies. Here, we make them for you. We also make truffles. It's easy."

Yes, easy, like planting onions in February, shearing sheep in March, making syrup in April, and then lambing in May. And after lambing come planting, weeding, cultivating, harvesting, and selling. It is the routine annual madness that has brought joy to Joel Rosen these last twenty seasons at Park Lake Farm. And it is his abiding pleasure to share it with customers like Jim and Joan, who understand its origins and purpose. While his link with people like the Halquists provides another dimension to his life, Jim says the same is true for him. His life is deepened by his relationship with Joel and Park Lake Farm.

Whereas Joel's farm life circles out to reach Ellery House, life at the bed and breakfast is uniquely urban. The Victorian Ellery House is on the edge of a deep wooded ravine just two blocks from Lake Superior. There are raccoon, deer, and occasionally, a bear in the ravine. But the Halquists can serve their guests breakfast, made all the better with Joel's maple syrup, and be in the city for sailing by late morning.

"Owning Ellery House has allowed us to have the gift of living and raising our children in Duluth," Jim says. It is a gift that they take pleasure in sharing with their guests.

Joel Rosen

JOAN'S STRAWBERRY RHUBARB MUFFINS

Makes 12 muffins

1¾ cups flour
½ cup sugar
2½ teaspoons baking powder
¾ teaspoon salt
1 egg, slightly beaten
¾ cup plain yogurt (milk can be substituted)
⅓ cup vegetable oil
½ teaspoon vanilla
¾ cup diced fresh rhubarb
1 cup chopped fresh strawberries

Preheat oven to 400°F. In a large bowl, mix flour, sugar, baking powder, and salt. In a small bowl, combine egg, yogurt, oil, and vanilla. Stir egg mixture into flour mixture just until all ingredients are moistened. Fold rhubarb and strawberries into batter.

Divide batter between 12 greased muffin cups. Sprinkle tops generously with sugar or glaze with Powdered Sugar Icing after baking. Bake in preheated oven at 400°F for 20 to 25 minutes or until golden brown.

POWDERED SUGAR ICING
½ lb. powdered sugar (about 2 cups)
2 to 3 tablespoons milk or half & half

In a large mixing bowl, combine powdered sugar with water until mixture is desired consistency. Add more water for a thinner consistency and less for a thicker consistency.

Makes approximately 1 cup glaze.

FEATHERBED EGGS

For this recipe, the Halquists use local farm-fresh eggs from free-range chickens.

1 slice of country French bread, ¾-inch thick
1 cup of extra-sharp cheddar cheese, grated
¼ cup diced ham (optional)
3 eggs
Half & half
Pepper, freshly ground

Cover bottom of buttered 1-quart casserole dish with one layer of country French bread. Tuck in bread pieces to fill any spaces. Cover with grated sharp cheddar. Sprinkle with diced ham. Mix eggs and half & half to make 1 cup of liquid (approximately ½ cup half & half). Drizzle egg/half & half mixture over top of cheese and ham. Grate pepper over the top. Cover and refrigerate overnight.

Put in cold oven and turn oven to 350°F. Bake, uncovered, for about 45 minutes until puffy and lightly golden.

JIM'S STUFFED FRENCH TOAST

4 cups country French bread, cut into ³/₄-inch cubes

6 oz. cream cheese, cut into ¹/₂-inch cubes

3 eggs

¹/₂ cup half & half

¹/₈ cup real maple syrup

3 tablespoons butter, melted

Layer half of the bread cubes in the bottom of a 1-quart buttered casserole dish. Scatter cream cheese cubes evenly over bread cubes. Cover with remaining bread cubes. Mix eggs, half & half, maple syrup, and melted butter. Drizzle over bread/cream cheese mixture.

Preheat oven to 350°F. Bake, uncovered, for 45 to 50 minutes, until top of cubes are golden brown. Serve with berry sauce and maple syrup.

MINNESOTA CHOCOLATE CAKE WITH CREAM CHEESE FROSTING

Makes one 9x13-inch pan or two 9-inch round cake pans

2 cups unbleached flour

1¹/₂ cups white sugar

¹/₂ cup unsweetened baking cocoa

1 teaspoon salt

1 tablespoon baking soda

1 cup buttermilk

1 cup brewed espresso or strong coffee

²/₃ cup canola oil

1 egg

1 teaspoon vanilla extract

Preheat oven to 350°F. In large mixing bowl, stir together flour, sugar, cocoa, salt, and soda. Add buttermilk, coffee, oil, egg, and vanilla. Beat until batter is smooth. (Batter will be thin.) Pour into greased cake pan(s).

Bake for about 30 minutes at 350°F or until cake tests done with a toothpick. Cool before frosting.

CREAM CHEESE FROSTING

12 oz. cream cheese

4 tablespoons soft, sweet cream butter (unsalted)

1 teaspoon vanilla extract

2¹/₂ cups powdered sugar

Juice from ¹/₂ lemon

In a medium mixing bowl, combine cream cheese, butter, vanilla extract, and powdered sugar; beat until smooth. Beat in lemon juice. Adjust vanilla, lemon juice, and powdered sugar to taste.

Frost cooled cake.

NEW SCENIC CAFÉ

Bay Produce

The menu at the New Scenic Café is affected, in part, by the migratory patterns of Lake Superior's herring, which move from the north shore to the south shore based on weather and seasonal patterns. Their behavior is not well understood by restaurant supply companies, but Scott Graden, New Scenic's chef and co-founder, has a close connection to those who bring him the silver fish. "I get herring from a couple of gentleman who fish out of Knife River, up the road from me—until the herring switch sides. Then I buy from Bodin's out of Bayfield on the south shore," Scott says.

Fish are important to the New Scenic, but so are a myriad of other local ingredients. Fortunately, Bay Produce's tomatoes aren't migratory. Each time the New Scenic staff heads into Duluth to pick up food from their favorite suppliers, they also cross the bridge and visit Bay Produce in Superior, Wisconsin.

During the twenty years that Bay Produce has been anchored in Superior, they have always delivered the quality insisted upon by Scott for his restaurant. Debbie Gergen, the director of Challenge Center, oversees twenty-five people who grow, prune, harvest, and pack the fruit from Bay Produce's ten thousand tomato plants. "There is a woman with cerebral palsy who works in the packing house," Debbie says. "She is probably the best packer on our staff when it comes to quality standards. If I ever pack with her, she'll slap my hands if I don't pack to the standards she wants."

Nailing down a definition for quality at the New Scenic is

Scott Graden

challenging. It has a Zen-ness to it, a sense one can taste but not exactly name. It might be captured in the excitement in the Bay Produce staff when they spy the first lemon-colored tomato blossom. Or perhaps it's reflected in the enthusiastic, "Here comes New Scenic, Here comes New Scenic!" that the packing crew occasionally shouts when the café's staff come down to visit Bay Produce's acre and a half of greenhouses.

"The New Scenic has experimented with a number of different tomato dishes," says Debbie, who also oversees shipping of tomatoes to large grocers, wholesalers, and small cafés. "When they were trying some green tomato dishes, we were able to provide them with what they needed. Not only have we been able to supply them with not-just-your-typical tomatoes, we've tried to accommodate their needs for any recipe they might be working on."

There is a pathway between Bay Produce employees carefully selecting—out of thousands—just the right green tomatoes and the quality of food brought to the tables for the delight of New Scenic diners. That's partly because Scott, Debbie, and their respective staffs refuse to accept the industrial model of food production as an end. Rather, fine taste, high levels of customer service, and meaningful work are ends, and the industrial models of efficiency and low cost are tools that can be adapted to meet those ends.

Another signpost on that path is an insistence on integrity. For example, diners and chefs alike enjoy the New Scenic's perennial and annual flower, plant, and herb garden, where fresh and functional herbs, such as tarragon, sage, rosemary, and chives, enhance their cooking and eating experiences. The herb garden was a collective effort of Lissa Ritchie Gardening (of Minnetonka), Scott, and his former business partner, Rita Bergstedt, after the café was purchased in 1999. The foliage transformed the front of the building and made the name "New Scenic" more honest, Scott notes.

"The herb garden is a value that's wrapped around the building," he says. "It greets our customers, like the smile on the server's face. It's a great place to wander; it makes people understand there are real people here getting their hands dirty. No corporation would do that." Picking herbs out the back door, or driving down the cold road in February to get vine-ripened tomatoes, allows Scott to obtain food that springs from the earth and the hands and minds of his neighborhood.

Scott's list of local suppliers is a yard long. He picks up fresh fruit from Sharri Zoff at Sharri's Berries. Louis Jenkins, a local poet, supplies him with mushrooms. Dave Rogotske, of Simple Gifts Syrup and Salmon, lives nearby and provides New Scenic with Alaskan King salmon and halibut. Another neighbor, Katie Hacker, brings in the eggs. Don Mount, of Clover Valley Forest Products, provides syrup. And Al's Dairy, a locally owned father and son operation, delivers Kemps dairy products. Although Kemps is a Minneapolis dairy, Al and his son are right down the road, and Scott likes to keep his money in the community.

Scott's customers and staff know that "right down the road" defines many of New Scenic's suppliers; it is, in part, the basis for their loyalty. So when New Scenic began serving Hawaiian Ahi tuna, some eyebrows were raised. "People have made comments like, 'why are you serving fish from Hawaii' or 'why don't you just have local lake trout?'" Scott notes. "It's an interesting dichotomy of values, because for as much as I want to eat as local as possible, my business strategy also includes offering foods that no one else does. Ahi is obviously not local, but the quality is there."

"Take my smoked duck breast as another example," Scott says. "I get the ducks from a Canadian company but have them processed by Eric Goerdt at Northern Waters Smokehaus in Duluth. We developed a brine and smoking

Scott Graden and Knife River fisherman Stephen Dahl

process, and he's been smoking duck for me every fall for the last four or five years. We worked together on it until we hit it right on the head."

So even the duck and the tuna come from hands connected to hearts, as well as heads, like those at Bay Produce, Al's Dairy, or the herb garden that replaced a parking lot. Out of those joined hands emerges a cuisine unique to the New Scenic Café that Scott calls American. It is American because it is unconfined, like jazz and rap, but also classical, like Copland. It's a culinary tune that, could they hear, would bring the herring back to the North Shore, and to the New Scenic Café, in a flash.

ORGANIC TOMATO AND HERB OIL APPETIZER

This is a great summer appetizer or salad course that couples well with artisan cheese and breads, as well as grilled foods. Enjoy with a crisp white wine, Burgundy Chardonnay, or Pinot Grigio.

2 large organic tomatoes
1 tablespoon cilantro oil
2 teaspoons white truffle oil
¼ cup microgreens
Sea salt and fresh ground pepper mélange to taste

Prepare the cilantro oil (below). Wash the tomatoes and slice into ¼-inch thick slices. Place them spiraling around a large plate or small platter. Drip the cilantro oil and truffle oil randomly over the tomatoes. Sprinkle with sea salt and freshly ground pepper mélange.

CILANTRO OIL

You could substitute almost any herb—such as chives or basil—for a different flavor.

½ lb. cilantro, washed well
½ cup olive oil
½ teaspoon kosher salt

Boil a small pot of water. Place ice and water in a small bowl. Plunge small bunches of cilantro in boiling water for 2 seconds. Remove and immediately plunge into the ice water; let cool.

Remove from the ice water and squeeze the water out. Cut the stems off and chop the leaves. Place in a food processor with the oil and salt and purée for 60 seconds. Place a strainer over a pitcher and scrape the cilantro mix into the strainer.

Let stand for 1 hour. Discard the solids; pour the oil into a small tube. Label, date, and refrigerate.

NORTHERN WATERS SMOKED SALMON APPETIZER

This dish would go nicely with an Alsace Riesling or Gewurztraminer. It can also be modified into a great salad by increasing the greens and tossing all of the ingredients together. Serve the baguette on the side.

Serves 6–8

8-oz. portion smoked salmon
4-oz. wheel of herbed Boursin cheese
1 cup mixed greens
½ Granny Smith apple

Roasted Garlic Vinaigrette (recipe below)
1 baguette

Slice the baguette into ¼-inch-thick pieces and toast in 350°F oven for 10 minutes. Toss the greens with a small amount of garlic vinaigrette. Slice the apple into thin half-moon slices.

Place greens in the center of plate. Place smoked salmon on one side and cheese on the other side. Place sliced apple in the center of greens. Arrange toasted baguette around the plate.

ROASTED GARLIC VINAIGRETTE

This recipe makes almost two cups of vinaigrette. Store in the refrigerator in a covered glass container.

1 cup garlic cloves, peeled and cleaned
½ cup balsamic vinegar
1 cup olive oil
¼ teaspoon cracked black pepper
1 chipotle pepper

Salt to taste

Roast garlic cloves on a sheet pan in a 300°F oven until garlic turns brown and starts to soften, about 30 minutes.

Place garlic, vinegar, black pepper, and the chipotle pepper in a food processor and process until smooth. Slowly add the olive oil, while the machine is running, to emulsify. Add salt as needed.

BITTERSWEET CHOCOLATE GANACHE FONDUE

½ cup heavy cream
½ cup dark bittersweet chocolate chips (about 70% cocoa)
½ cup strawberries
3 kiwi
1 banana
Other seasonal local fruit
½ cup whipped cream
3 oz. Camembert cheese

Bring the cream to a slow boil. Place the chocolate chips in a large dry bowl. Pour the hot cream over the chips. Stir until smooth and keep warm until ready to use.

In mixer, whip heavy cream until stiff peaks form. Add 1 tablespoon sugar, if sweetened cream is desired. Cut the fruit and cheese into 1-inch chunks. Pour the chocolate ganache into a fondue bowl. Place the fondue bowl on a serving plate and surround with the fruit and cheese. Place dollops of whipped cream on fruit. Serve with skewers or fondue forks for dipping.

PINE AND LAKE COUNTRY

PRAIRIE BAY RESTAURANT

The Farm on St. Mathias

"The whole food scene is changing," says Prairie Bay Chef Matt Annand, "and we're trying to be on the forefront up here." "Up here" is Baxter, Minnesota. The forefront is a synthesis of made-from-scratch Minnesota classics influenced by Matt's experience at New York's Culinary Institute, restaurants in Napa Valley and Arizona, and his extensive international travel.

Prairie Bay's tuna noodle hot dish is an example of a Minnesota-classic makeover. It's Asian-inspired with seared Ahi tuna on top of soba noodles. It has a lot of cilantro, fresh ginger, bell peppers, and chiles. "While we try to be fun and inventive, there's nothing crazy or over-intellectualized," Matt says. "I grew up north of here and I have a pretty good idea what people will eat. I know we're pushing things a little; however, people are becoming more interested in food."

One influence that is changing people's perception of food is the coming-of-age of television cooking shows. "It's kind of ridiculous," Matt says. "You become a chef so you can hide in the kitchen, and then they put chefs on television."

While one aspect of Matt's personality cringes at the thought of televised kitchen melodrama, another delights in performance cooking. Prairie Bay features a chef's bar, which allows eight diners to look into the eye of the kitchen's storm and be served specially prepared dishes.

When people come to the chef's bar, Matt asks them if they have any dietary restrictions, food allergies, or foods they

Matt Annand

dislike. Being sure to avoid those things, he and his cooks then put their talent to work. "It's fun for the customers to watch cooks create on the fly," Matt says. "We always do different things—we'll take menu items and transform them—incorporating whatever is in season.

"It keeps our cooks interested and gets their creative juices flowing," Matt continues. "People want to see the chef and I like to talk to people. They want to know what's coming up on the menu and what the recipe is. We share those, but we don't actually work with many recipes except when we're baking. We cook by technique, so we'll jot that down along with a basic recipe to follow."

Bob and Arlene Jones

Cooking by technique, cooking from scratch, and performance cooking are parts of the recipe that Matt believes will keep Prairie Bay out in the forefront—along with buying the freshest, tastiest local ingredients.

Matt orders daily from his list of local farmers and producers. He'll call Bill Linder for shiitake, wild-crafted mushrooms, and duck. He'll call Forest Mushrooms, out of St. Joseph, for his other mushrooms. A woman a few miles up the road gets a call when he needs asparagus in the spring. And he's got The Farm on St. Mathias' number memorized.

"I started sourcing local food one farmer at a time, and The Farm on St. Mathias was among the first," Matt says. "The farmer-chef dynamic is more than about simply selling and purchasing food. It is about forming a relationship and trust. The Farm on St. Mathias and Prairie Bay has grown together, learned from one another and we've inspired each other.

"Prairie Bay decided from the start that we were going to support our community, period. We've set up shop here in the lakes area, and our business model largely incorporates the philosophy of giving back to succeed. Food just happens to be our medium." The region's first food truck, Prairie Bay's The Side Dish (local-motive kitchen), is a natural extension of that mission.

Beginning with locally grown foods, The Farm and Prairie Bay have forged a partnership that now includes an annual wine dinner at the farm and weddings at the farm, and they have even partnered in showcasing The Side Dish at local farmers' markets. In a unique partnership, The Farm on St. Mathias and Prairie Bay Restaurant continue to delight increasingly discriminating consumers with distinctive local heirloom tomatoes, potatoes, mushrooms, herbs, and year-round greens.

For The Farm's owners, Bob and Arlene Jones, engaging communities in the importance of knowing where their food comes from is step one; using agriculture to reconnect consumers with the source of their food, linking consumers back to the land, is the goal. Starting with a CSA and an on-farm market stand, the Joneses have grown The Farm into a premiere destination and educational farm. Because of the success of partnerships such as Prairie Bay's, The Farm has launched SPROUT MN, a Central Minnesota Food Hub, working with a large network of small family farms to source locally grown food.

"My focus in our kitchens has now largely shifted from hours of searching and sourcing into growing and improving. SPROUT MN is becoming the one-stop shop for all that is local, and not only have our customers benefited, but our entire region is so much better for it."

The chef-producer fusion has led to many successes in the region. Prairie Bay and The Farm on St. Mathias continue to stand at the forefront of the food and agricultural scene.

PRAIRIE BAY PIZZA MARGHERITA

FRESH AND EASY PIZZA DOUGH
Yield: 2 14-inch pizza circles

¼-oz. package active dry yeast
1 teaspoon sugar
1 cup warm water
1 tablespoon extra virgin olive oil
3½ cups all-purpose flour
1 teaspoon kosher salt

In a bowl, combine yeast, sugar, and water and let sit for 8 to 10 minutes; stir in olive oil.

In a food processor, combine flour and salt for 10 seconds. Add the liquid mixture a little at a time while processing, until a ball is formed that isn't sticky. Add a little more flour if necessary.

Remove dough from processor and knead by hand for 3 to 5 minutes. Place in an oiled bowl and cover. Put in a warm place to rise for an hour, or until doubled in size.

Cut in half and roll (or press) each half into ¼- to ⅛-inch thickness, or approximately a 14-inch circle. Place on pizza screen or lightly floured baking stone.

ROASTED GARLIC CLOVES
1 large garlic bulb
1 teaspoon butter
Salt
Stock or water

Preheat oven to 350°F. In a small container or pan using a double-layered "nest" of aluminum foil, place garlic in oven with butter, a little salt, and stock or water. Cover completely and bake for 45 minutes. Uncover and bake for 10 to 15 minutes more. Cut the very top off the bulb and squeeze to remove roasted cloves.

PIZZA SAUCE
Yield: 2 to 2½ cups

2 cloves garlic, crushed
1 medium onion, diced small
2 tablespoons extra virgin olive oil
28-oz. can Italian plum tomatoes or 5 to 6
    seasonal/ripe fresh tomatoes
Pinch cayenne
1 tablespoon sugar
Kosher salt to taste
10 to 12 basil stems, whole (leaves reserved)

In a heavy-bottomed saucepan, sweat onions and garlic in olive oil over low to medium heat until onions become translucent and garlic is very fragrant.

Crush tomatoes and drain well. Add to pan with sugar and cayenne. Season with salt. Cook over medium heat for 15 minutes, stirring occasionally. Add basil stems (reserving leaves for pizza topping) and cook another 5 to 10 minutes. Sauce should be broken down. Do not purée. Remove basil stems and adjust seasonings to taste.

PIZZA ASSEMBLY
2 14-inch Fresh and Easy Pizza Dough circles
Pizza Sauce
½ bulb Roasted Garlic
Sliced tomatoes
1 cup shredded mozzarella cheese
6 to 12 basil leaves
½ cup grated Parmesan
1 tablespoon extra virgin olive oil
1 teaspoon fresh ground black pepper

Preheat oven to 450°. Spread sauce over pizza, leaving a half-inch border around outside. Sprinkle roasted garlic cloves, sliced tomatoes, and mozzarella uniformly. Bake on the bottom rack for 10 to 15 minutes or until the top and crust are golden brown. Top with basil leaves, olive oil, and fresh ground pepper.

WILD MUSHROOM STRUDEL

This strudel is very versatile—use as an appetizer, a brunch dish, or as a side with any entrée, especially game. Great paired with the Sweet Corn Polenta.

Yield: 8 strudels

Canola or neutral cooking oil (as needed)

4 cups brushed and cleaned medium mushrooms, chopped (whatever is in season)

¼ cup Roasted Garlic Cloves; use the same method as used with Margherita Pizza

1 medium onion, diced small

2 bunches (about 4 to 5 cups) cleaned, stemmed spinach

1 tablespoon water

½ cup chevre (goat cheese)

¾ tablespoon lavender flowers, finely chopped (or fresh thyme or rosemary)

1 cup finely grated Parmesan cheese

1 sprig rosemary, finely chopped

Salt and pepper to taste

16 sheets phyllo dough

½ cup melted butter

White truffle oil, for garnish (optional)

STUFFING

Season each step with just a little salt to enhance flavor.

Preheat a sauté pan over medium to high heat, add a little oil and then the dry mushrooms. Sear dry mushrooms for 3 to 5 minutes. Remove. Add 1 tablespoon oil and caramelize onions over medium heat for 5 minutes. Remove. Lower heat and add spinach along with 1 tablespoon water until spinach is wilted. Remove and drain spinach, pressing any residue liquid out. Combine all cooked ingredients in a bowl with chevre, roasted garlic, lavender, Parmesan, rosemary, salt, and pepper.

ASSEMBLY

Preheat oven to 400°F. Working quickly to keep delicate sheets from drying out, brush 1 full sheet of dough with melted butter and place another sheet directly over the top. Brush again. Fold in half and brush again, fold in half one more time and brush again. You should now have 8 layers. Place approximately 1/2 cup of stuffing toward the bottom of the rectangle. Fold ends up close and roll tightly to eliminate air pockets. Brush outside with butter. Repeat with remaining sheets and filling.

Precut into pieces of desired size before baking or keep whole. Bake 6 to 10 minutes or until golden brown outside and hot inside. Garnish with white truffle oil.

BACKLOT BISTRO SWEET CORN POLENTA

Makes one 9x11-inch pan

1 cup corn meal
1½ cups chicken stock
1 cup heavy cream
1 cup fresh sweet corn kernels
1 tablespoon kosher salt, check seasoning before baking
1 tablespoon fresh thyme or rosemary, chopped
Herbs, roasted mushrooms, and fresh corn, for garnish

In a heavy-bottomed saucepan, add cream and stock. Slowly bring to a simmer while sprinkling in corn meal. Whisk constantly to prevent sticking. Add 1 cup sweet corn, salt, and chopped thyme or rosemary. Lower heat and stir with a wooden spoon for about 15 minutes until mixture is very thick and is no longer "grainy" when tasting.

Spread onto a lightly greased, rimmed cookie sheet or baking pan to an even depth of up to two inches. Refrigerate for at least one hour. Cut into diamonds or any desired shape.

Fry top-side down in a lightly greased sauté pan until golden brown. Flip to warm through.

Garnish with herbs, roasted mushrooms, and fresh corn.

BREWED AWAKENINGS
COFFEEHOUSE

Spica Farm

Things often don't turn out the way people expect. Take Joan Foster of Grand Rapids as an example. She had a good year-round job with Headstart, until Congress cut funding and her summer hours were eliminated. She found herself laid off with time on her hands.

Joan's son was sixteen at the time, and teenagers often have impractical ideas that adults should listen to more carefully. Thankfully, in Joan's case, she did. "My son was encouraging me to open a coffee shop," she recalls. "Then, our local cooperative grocery store offered me free rent if I started a coffee shop in the front of the store. How could I turn that down?"

Thus was born Brewed Awakenings, a name coined from the fertile mind of a teenage friend of Joan's son. Soon, Joan and her son set about serving coffee to the co-op's customers. It went well; co-op sales improved. But then summer was over, Joan's son headed off to the arts magnet high school in Minneapolis, and the Headstart job opened up again.

"I fully intended to go back to my job in the fall," Joan says. But she didn't. Now, more than ten years after that fateful summer, travelers on U.S. Highway 2 into Grand Rapids see a sign promoting Brewed Awakenings vegetarian soups. Joan and her husband have moved the coffee shop, for the second time,

Joan Foster

into their own building with a seating capacity of seventy-seven.

That's how life can be. It takes surprising turns as it unfolds. Laurie and Brad Jones can testify to that. Laurie's a public health nurse for Itasca County; Brad's a forester. But they both share a love of horticulture, so they bought a farm on the Swan River not far from Grand Rapids. "We were just going to raise enough food for ourselves," says Brad.

But nature has a way of providing surplus, and the human mind has a way of responding generously. Nowadays, Brad and Laurie's Spica Farm provides a few custom-processed steers to customers who appreciate grass-fed beef. They also grow durham wheat for people who enjoy grinding their own flour for bread. And they deliver vegetables weekly to Brewed Awakenings, when the seasons allow it.

"Customers at Brewed Awakenings know us through our food," Brad says. "It's a cornerstone business in the community because it connects a lot of people." A connection that, from time to time, gets broadcasted over the airwaves. "We have a community radio station in Grand Rapids," Brad says, "and sometimes I'll hear the announcer say, 'I just saw so-and-so down at the coffee shop.'"

Spica Farm vegetables regularly find their way into Joan's fabulous soups—soups that lure new and old customers to the table at Brewed Awakenings. A fall favorite is Golden Autumn soup made with tomato, apple, and orange juices blended together with squash.

"I got that idea out of the *Sundays at the Moosewood Cookbook*," Joan explains. The Moosewood cookbooks have been an inspiration to Joan. "I never would have thought those three juices could be combined, but they're delicious together," she says. "I turned the Moosewood recipe, a purée called Autumn Gold, into more of a stew with potatoes and celery and named it Golden Autumn." With that same base she makes Golden Bean soup.

"When I started making soups in the co-op grocery, I never wrote any recipes down," she continues. "I'd just walk around the store to see what looked good. One day I'd have soup with rice and beans, the next I'd have pasta, and then I'd have potatoes with something else. It was fun cooking there. They had a huge spice rack that I'd look at and say, 'O-oh-h, this would be good in soup.'"

Joan has compiled a recipe book with the fifty-five original soup recipes from Brewed Awakenings. The soups don't get served in a regular rotation because she likes to take advantage of local, seasonal, and surplus produce; and she obliges customers who lobby for their favorites. "My tomato coconut curry gets served more often because people who have had it really want to have it again," Joan says. "But with seating for seventy-seven people instead of twenty-two, I can make more than one soup a day. Later in the day, we refrigerate any leftover soup for people to take home. A lot of people have allergies, so I want to make sure I have two or three choices."

And Joan isn't stopping at fifty-five soups. There are others emerging. Spica Farm's CSA (community supported agriculture) subscription has had a noted effect on new recipe development. If, for instance, there is a lot of kale in a week's delivery, Joan may create a kale soup. If the ingredients to a new recipe don't quite work out, she'll alter it a little the next time.

The recipe evolves, just like life. You never know how it's going to turn out.

Laurie and Brad Jones

TOMATO COCONUT CURRY SOUP

This soup is very good without the toppings, but the toppings make for a nice presentation and add even more flavor.

Serves 4–6

1¾ quarts fresh tomatoes; chop ¾ quart and puree 1 quart in the blender
Or use:
28 oz. can tomato sauce
28 oz. can diced tomatoes

1½ cups carrots, sliced thin
¾ to 1 tablespoon yellow curry paste; start with the lesser amount and add to taste, this curry is hot!
1 teaspoon salt, adjust as needed
2 cloves minced garlic
⅛ cup apricot preserves
½ cup unsweetened shredded coconut

In a large saucepan or Dutch oven, add ingredients in the order given. Bring to a simmer, and cook until the carrots are tender. Adjust curry and salt, to taste.

Garnish, if you like, with plain unflavored yogurt and chopped chives.

GERMAN POTATO STEW

4 large potatoes, chopped
1 medium onion, chopped
14.5-oz. can sauerkraut (approximately 2 cups)
½ lb. fresh or frozen green beans, cut into bite-sized pieces
Scant tablespoon dry dill or 3 tablespoons fresh dill
½ teaspoon black pepper, freshly ground
3 tablespoons flour
6 oz. sour cream
6 oz. plain unflavored yogurt

Clean and chop potatoes and place in a large saucepan or Dutch oven. Cover with hot water. Bring to a simmer and cook until the potatoes are tender, about 20 minutes. Add the next 4 ingredients. Add more hot water if needed to cover.

In a separate bowl, mix the flour into the sour cream until smooth. Add the sour cream and yogurt to soup. Heat thoroughly and serve.

POTATO SPINACH SOUP

Serves 6

3 cups potatoes, diced
1 large onion, chopped
½ teaspoon salt
¼ teaspoon lemon pepper
1 tablespoon fresh basil, chopped
1½ teaspoons fresh rosemary, chopped, or ½ teaspoon dried
1½ teaspoons fresh thyme, chopped, or ½ teaspoon dried
¼ cup fresh parsley, chopped

½ lb. fresh spinach, chopped
2 ounces cream cheese
½ cup grated Parmesan cheese
½ cup grated cheddar cheese

Put 5 cups hot water in a large saucepan. Add the first seven ingredients. Simmer until potatoes are tender, about 20 minutes. Add water if needed. Add the rest of the ingredients. Heat and stir until cheese is melted. Salt and pepper to taste.

COUNTRY BED & BREAKFAST

Steve Anderson Sugarbush

Nestled on thirty-five acres of fields and woods just north of Shafer and a short five-mile drive west of historic Taylors Falls is the Country Bed & Breakfast. Lois Barott and her husband Kenneth (Budd) began the B&B in 1982. After Budd's passing in 1999, daughter Sally moved home to the rural countryside to continue the business with her mother.

Visitors are greeted by a large and gracious 130-year-old red brick farmhouse with a spacious deck, gardens, and walking paths leading into the nearby woods. Upstairs, the three guestrooms—the Lavender Room, the Green Room, and the Old Attic Room—are comfortably furnished.

Lois's family moved to the sixty-acre farm in 1938 when she was ten years old. It was still a working farm then, although only the stone foundation of the barn remained. "We had nowhere to put the cows," Lois says, "so we milked them outside."

Then Lois's father and grandfather acquired an old barn from Center City, which had been the livery stable for the Methodist Church. They took it down piece by piece and rebuilt the barn. "That's the existing barn today," Lois explains. "I've had some restoration done to it these past five years by Al Hawkinson. He's a high school classmate of Sally's who specializes in restoring

Lois and Sally Barott

old barns and buildings. It's been a lot of fun, and the restoration continues."

Sally has been researching the history of the farm since the early 1970s. "Only two families have lived here," she says. "The Lars and Ingre Thorsander family and our family. Lars and Ingre came from Småland, Sweden, in 1869 during the famine."

Sally is a Swedish immigrant historian as well as the B&B's marketing and advertising manager. "My grandparents bought the home from the Thorsander family in 1938 and my parents bought it from my grandparents in 1965," she continues. "I have many wonderful memories growing up here with my five siblings. When my parents turned it into a B&B in 1982, we all had to come home and clean out the attic and closets to make space for the guest rooms."

Country Bed & Breakfast has been in operation for twenty-five years. The concept began in the late 1970s after Lois and Budd took a few trips to Sweden. Lois says, "We modeled our B&B on the European-style B&Bs that share their homes with traveling guests each night. The family lives in the home and the guests 'live' that family's culture."

Lois and Sally love telling family stories around the kitchen breakfast table. They know the rhythm and pacing of each of the stories and together weave them into a complete tapestry. With appreciative and loquacious guests, the conversation flows as easily as the Swedish Egg Kaffe (coffee) at their memorable breakfasts. When Lois is serving her buttermilk pancakes, which are so light they nearly float off the plate, she'll tell about her cousin Steve Anderson, in nearby Center City, who provides the maple syrup.

"Steve has been making maple syrup for nearly fifty years," Lois says, as she passes a golden liquid that adds value to her already valuable pancakes. To get Steve's syrup, Lois and Sally have to go visit him. That's what many people in the area do, including WCCO radio and a national television show.

Steve will tell you that he has 1,200 taps. "Sometimes you've got to have that many," he says. "You put three pails on a tree and only one of them may run. I think I should have a stethoscope when I go out there and tap them."

Steve laughs gently when he says stethoscope. He wants to be clear to city-folk this is a joke. There are other mysteries in the sugar bush. In his half century of collecting sap, Steve has experienced a lot of them. One thing he's learned is that he can't predict whether it will be a good year or not.

"I'll give you your forecast on the 15th of April," he says. "It'll be all over with. It isn't any different than putting in 1,000 acres of corn. Is it going to be a good crop or a poor crop? You'll know in October, but not May."

Steve has a particular disdain for prognosticators who make the early season predictions. "I know one year Harold and I were tapping. It was 1977," he says, checking his book of records, which he's kept since the 1960s. "1976 was really a dry summer. On the radio they were saying, those trees are going to die. You can't tap them. We started believing those radio people. We almost thought they knew what they were talking about. It's like anything else on the radio. You don't know if it's . true or not."

It wasn't true.

That year when Steve and Harold tapped the trees and started cooking, they worked steady for a month. "Those trees, it didn't matter what the weather did," Steve recalls. "The ground was so dry they said the trees were going to die, you know. It got cool at night. It got warm in the day. The sun shone. It was raining. It didn't make a nickel's worth of difference. Those trees were nuts. We couldn't catch up. It was unbelievable."

After all that, after the best season in half a century, those trees produced sap the next season, too. Some of them are still making sap thirty years later. Steve doesn't know which are stranger: the radio prognosticators making endless predictions, right or wrong, or the trees and their cycles.

He does know that being in the sugar bush for the sap run is a fine thing. He's seventy years old, and he'll likely continue the annual harvest as long as he can. "It's a good place to be in the spring," he says. "Everything is coming to life. You've been boarded up in the house. Then you go out there and the birds are singing and the sun is nice."

But Steve's syrup-cooking partner, Harold Vitalis, passed away five years ago. Something is absent from the brightness of spring that Steve so enjoys, now. He'd made syrup with Harold for more than forty springs and had known Harold since he was five years old.

"We prided ourselves in making fancy syrup instead of making it look dark," Steve says. "I miss my partner."

It's this amber pride of Steve and Harold's sugar bush that Lois and Sally Barott take pleasure in pouring over their morning buttermilk pancakes at the Country Bed & Breakfast.

Steve Anderson

BUDD'S COUNTRY BED & BREAKFAST OMELET

The brown eggs are from Karl and Kris Ruser, Center City; the cucumbers are from the farmer's market in Lindstrom; and the herbs and vegetables are from Sally Barott's herb garden, all organic. The cheese is from Eichten's in Center City.

4 tablespoons margarine
2 tablespoons chopped onion
2 tablespoons chopped green pepper
2 tablespoons chopped fresh mushrooms
3 farm-fresh eggs
1 tablespoon cold water
1 oz. Gouda cheese, grated
1 oz. mild cheddar cheese, grated
Salt and pepper to taste

Heat an omelet pan on high. Add 4 tablespoons of margarine and melt (use margarine, it handles the higher temperature, butter will burn). Add the chopped vegetables and sauté over medium heat until tender, about 3 minutes. In a small bowl, beat the eggs with a fork for 30 seconds. Add the water and continue to beat for another 15 seconds. Add the eggs to the sautéed vegetables. As they cook, pull the eggs away from the sides of the pan. Continue until the omelet is firm enough to flip. Flip with a large spatula and heat the other side of the omelet. Sprinkle the grated cheeses onto the omelet. Fold over the other half to melt the cheese. Salt and pepper to taste.

Garnish with a fresh tomato slice, fresh cucumber slice, chopped chives, and a parsley sprig. Serve immediately.

LOIS'S BUTTERMILK PANCAKES

The maple syrup is from Steve Anderson, Lois's cousin in Center City.

2½ cups unbleached flour
2½ tablespoons baking powder
¼ cup granulated sugar
1 teaspoon salt
3 farm-fresh eggs
2 cups buttermilk (shake the carton well before measuring)
2 teaspoons vanilla

In a large bowl, mix the dry ingredients together. Add the eggs, buttermilk, and vanilla. Mix with on medium speed until the batter is smooth, about 2 minutes. Using a ¼ cup, pour pancakes onto a preheated cast iron griddle that has been oiled with shortening. A non-stick griddle will also work. Flip the pancakes over when the top starts to bubble. Heat the other side until golden brown.

Serve with fresh country butter and homemade maple syrup.

RED RIVER VALLEY

CARIBOU GRILL

Double J Elk

Build it and they will come. Nobody takes that little phrase seriously. Nobody, that is, except some people in Hallock, population 1,200, in far northwestern Minnesota.

"Since we opened in January 2004, it's been busy a lot for lunches, on the weekend, and in the evening when there is an event in town," says Kristen Blomquist, one of the co-owners of Hallock's Caribou Grill. "I think people come because the food is good. They drive over from North Dakota, and we also have friends who come from forty-five miles away."

Friends and neighbors are far apart in Kittson County, where Hallock is the county seat, so forty-five miles may not be a vast distance. But the Caribou Grill offers rewards not available in other small-town restaurants and cafes. Rewards such as grilled, baked, or blackened salmon fillets; a porterhouse pork chop; a pork tenderloin covered in cream sauce with mushrooms and peppers; or scaloppine with rainbow fettuccini topped with artichoke hearts and mushrooms in a rich, creamy sauce.

"Our cook, Dawn Lindstrom, is great," Kristen says. "She's more of a home-cooking kind of a cook, not a trained chef. We've tried trained chefs and they tended to have an attitude." One of the issues that those trained chefs had an attitude about was using local ingredients. Their training, Kristen says, led them to prefer standardized units of commoditized food off the back of a corporate food service truck.

Serving up elk steaks at Caribou Grill

But that's not the preferred culinary methodology up north at the Caribou Grill.

"In the summer, Dean, our gardener, will bring in produce for Dawn to use," Kristen explains. "In our first year, our manager and our cooks were not into it. They wanted to predict what they were going to get. But Dean might come in with 10 pounds of green beans, or the green beans he thought would be ripe weren't, so he'll bring in something else. With this system, we know the quality is better than what comes off the truck, but we have to adjust our menu to what's available."

But when Dean's green beans, zucchini, or tomatoes are ripe, they will end up in one of Dawn's homemade soups. She makes two or three soups a day and is famous for them. "My favorite is her tomato," says Kristen. "It's got really chunky bits of tomato in it. Some of the others are clam chowder, pea soup, potato soup, chicken dumpling—she makes her own dumplings—and chicken and rice."

Another occasional rewards that locals and long-distance travelers can enjoy are elk burgers, chili, and steaks.

"Dawn has a secret recipe for making the elk burgers at the Caribou Grill," says Jerod Hanson, whose family raises elk in rural Hallock. Jerod got into elk farming in 1999 as a way to earn some extra income. Although bull-antler velvet and breeding stock have been the mainstays of the small United States elk industry, Jerod chose to focus on sales of meat. In addition to selling ground meat, he sells steaks like ribeye, New York strip, and sirloin. Elk dishes are not regularly on the menu at the Caribou Grill because Jerod cannot keep up with the demand. The fact that they are there at all puts the restaurant on equal footing with some pretty upscale urban eateries.

Elk meat is known for its great taste, but in the U.S. it is rare. When it is available, it is often imported frozen from New Zealand. For many years, domestic elk were so valuable as breeding stock that they were rarely sold for their meat. However, times have changed and elk meat is currently competitive with all natural or organically grown beef and has the benefit of being lower in fat and cholesterol.

That's good for diners at the Caribou Grill. It's also fine with Jerod because it creates a niche for his farm's product. He likes raising elk because they don't require as much labor as beef cattle. In addition to their low maintenance requirements, they also use pasture more efficiently. But Jerod, like all livestock farmers in northwestern Minnesota, suffers from a lack of processing facilities. When he's ready to convert living elk into ribeye and chili, he has to take the animal almost 150 miles to a small plant in Barnesville.

It's possible the region could support another small meat-processing plant. After all, Kristen and her business partners built a fine-dining restaurant on the northern prairie and the diners did come. They came as individuals and in groups, for employee Christmas parties and political party meetings, for a drink at the bar and to listen to Miss North Dakota sing in the lounge. And while making the business work financially hasn't been easy, Kristen and her partners have built a community resource appreciated by people for miles around.

STRAWBERRY SPINACH SALAD

Serves 8

16 cups fresh spinach, washed and torn into
 bite-sized pieces
4 cups fresh strawberries, sliced
½ cup fresh bacon, fried, drained, and in small pieces
½ cup slivered almonds, toasted
½ cup Parmesan cheese, shredded
4 eggs, hard-boiled and cut in chunks

Combine all ingredients and serve with a raspberry vinaigrette dressing.

Bluefin Bay of Tofte, Minnesota, makes a good raspberry vinaigrette, which is readily available. You can also add bite-sized pieces of roasted chicken to this salad.

BARBECUE BACON ELK BURGER

This is so unexpectedly delicious in its simplicity.
 1 serving

⅓ lb. ground elk, formed into a patty
Salt and pepper to taste
1 slice cheddar cheese
2 slices onion, fried
2 slices smoky bacon, fried
1 tablespoon of your favorite BBQ sauce
1 multi-grain bun, buttered and toasted
Lettuce, tomato, and pickles to garnish

Separately fry the onions and bacon to desired doneness. Sprinkle salt and pepper on both sides of the burger and rub it in. Grill the elk burger, and toast the bun while the meat is being grilled. Elk is low-fat, so try not to overcook for best flavor. Add the cheese to the hot burger about a minute after turning; cook another couple of minutes and remove from the heat.

Put the burger on the bun, add bacon, sauce, onion, and other garnish, and enjoy.

CORN CHOWDER

Serves 8–10

1 small onion
2 ribs celery, diced
¼ cup red pepper, diced
¼ cup green pepper, diced
1 clove garlic, minced
2 russet potatoes, diced
2 cups fresh shucked corn (frozen will work in the off season)
1 quart chicken stock
1 quart milk
½ cup butter

½ cup flour
Salt, pepper, and chopped fresh parsley to taste

Melt the butter and sauté all vegetables, except the corn and potatoes, until the onions are translucent. Sprinkle flour over the vegetables and continue cooking for one minute, stirring constantly. Slowly add the stock and milk, stirring constantly. Add corn, potatoes, and seasonings. Simmer for 20 minutes, stirring often. Salt and pepper to taste, garnish with chopped parsley.

WILD HARE BISTRO
& COFFEEHOUSE

Farmucopia

When you step in to the Wild Hare Bistro, you're transported to a warm world unlike any other in northwest Minnesota—and that's how co-owners Moni Schneider, Reed Olson, and Norwood Hall want you to feel. It could be a frigid January day out, but inside, the walls are squarely hung with the month's featured art, each table of friends seems to know at least one other, and the orchestra of steamers' whirs and knife slices betrays the remarkable amount of fresh, delicious fare crossing the counter.

Transporting hardy customers without a need for wheels or wings is what this team excels at. With a combined forty years of cooking experience—from coordinating food services at a nearby language immersion camp to preparing dishes in remote Alaskan makeshift kitchens—the folks behind the scenes are "providing something that wasn't there," as Moni puts it: "fresh, healthy food with an ethnic flair." In her various roles over fifteen years at Concordia Language Villages, people often asked her to bring her culturally diverse meals to the public, but it wasn't until an acquaintance was in need that the Wild Hare was born. When their friend, Carolyn, lost her husband, she also lost her desire to run their café alone, but she wanted to make sure their dream lived on after he passed away. That's when Moni, her husband, Norwood, and their business partner Reed jumped in.

"It was a bit impulsive," Moni says. "It was the right first step, but I would love a real kitchen." It's been nearly ten years

Moni Schneider, Norwood F. Hall II, and Reed Olson

now. Coffee and tea are expected at a cafe, but the daily salads and from-scratch soups are what make this a bistro and sets it apart from other restaurants in town. In season, those dishes hold fresh produce from local farmers, such as Mike Schumacher and Marina Lovell from nearby Farmucopia. The menu for the day's salad reads deceptively vague, so whatever is harvested can go in without much fanfare, be it radish, carrot, cucumber, or lettuce. "Going local was really easy," Moni

says, before laughing at how producers offered their products to them early on. Even customers brought in produce if they had a bumper crop.

Mike and Marina provided the Wild Hare with a CSA share for several years before all parties realized a more direct model would make the most sense. "A couple of years ago, we figured out they were getting stuff they didn't necessarily use in their recipes. Now, with the relationship we've establish, they know when I'm coming to town and what I grow and can put in an order," Marina says.

Their farm, located on eighty acres of rolling fields and forest about a half hour from town, is certified organic and completely off-grid. They "walk the walk," extending their concern about the environment and energy they use to every aspect of their lives, from the food they provide their share members each year to how they supply water to their plants, chickens, draft ponies, and self-built straw-bale house with a solar-powered pump.

"Becoming certified has been very important for us," Mike says, "not only for the soil and our customers, but also for our organizational purposes." Although the initial application was quite a bit of work, it sets up a system of tracking that helps them be the best land stewards they can be. The conservation easement on their forested acreage carries that same attention to detail from the fields to the woods.

With about thirty CSA customers, Marina feels they've found a good balance. "We're not such a big operation that we lose touch with our customers," she says. And Moni at the Wild Hare couldn't agree more. "This community and this work bring us closer to our neighbors. We help each other. Staff can contribute in a more team-oriented way because they can see what it takes to bring everything together." Everyone involved seems to thrive on collaboration, creativity, and resourcefulness.

Red Lake rice takes a starring role in a lunch favorite: the wild rice salad sandwich. Their bestseller is a chicken salad sandwich with apricot curry spread. Moni decides what the specials will be on the menu that day based on what she can get her hands on. Root vegetables, such as Elvin's potatoes and Farmucopia's carrots, are turned into soups that warm customers' bellies during the winter months, while salads are composed of fresh, local veggies from Memorial Day into autumn, as long as there's enough.

Despite the lack of kitchen space, the team at the Wild Hare—and the farmers behind them—seems to find ways to meet customer's desires. Usually, it's just breakfast and lunch. But during monthly First Friday art walks, they open their doors for dinner, much to their customers' satisfaction. To spice up the winter months, the meal takes on a specific ethnic theme. During the warm summer days, local produce and regional traditions are front and center. Year round, they live up to their motto of "world flavors, local flair."

KOHLRABI CRÈME SOUP

2 tablespoons butter (or olive oil)

$^1/_2$ large yellow onion, diced (about $^1/_2$ pound or 1 cup)

$1^1/_2$ lb. kohlrabi, peeled of their thick outer layer and cut into a $^1/_2$-inch dice

1 cup medium gold potato, peeled and cut into a $^1/_2$-inch dice

4 large cloves garlic, sliced

2 tablespoons fresh tarragon, or $^1/_2$ teaspoon dried tarragon

$4^1/_2$ cups low-sodium chicken or vegetable broth

$^1/_4$ cup half & half

Small handful fresh spinach leaves, torn (about $^1/_2$ cup)

1 oz. fresh goat cheese (optional)

Salt and pepper to taste

2 teaspoons olive oil

4 slices baguette, cubed

Scallions or chives and Aleppo pepper, to garnish

Heat butter in a heavy-bottomed stock pot. Add diced onion and kohlrabi. Sauté until edges begin to brown. Add potatoes and garlic, sauté 2 to 3 minutes, until garlic is fragrant. Add broth or water to cover. If using dried tarragon, add it now. Simmer the contents, covered, until kohlrabi is soft, about 30 minutes.

Heat 2 teaspoons of olive oil in a skillet. Once hot, add bread cubes and fry until golden and crisp. Reserve.

Once kohlrabi has softened, turn off the heat and add half & half, spinach, fresh tarragon, and goat cheese, if using. Allow to cool slightly, until spinach is wilted. Carefully transfer contents to a blender in two batches. Cover tightly with blender lid and a dish towel. Hold lid firmly closed while slowly blending into a smooth puree. Garnish soup with crispy croutons, scallions or chives, and a generous pinch of Aleppo pepper.

MASHED POTATO CAKES WITH BRAISED KALE

1½ lb. red-skinned potatoes, peeled and cut into 1-inch cubes
  (3 cups)

2 teaspoons sliced scallions or chives

1 oz. parmesan, shredded

1 oz. fresh goat cheese

1 egg

2 teaspoons flour

Salt and pepper to taste

4 slices thick-cut bacon

½ sweet onion, diced small (¾ cup)

3 cloves garlic, sliced

1 bunch lacinato kale, about 12 large leaves, stemmed and
  chopped coarsely

½ cup chicken or vegetable broth

1 teaspoon maple syrup

2 teaspoons dried currants

Salt and pepper to taste

2 teaspoons toasted pine nuts

4 teaspoons sour cream or plain Greek yogurt

Preheat oven to 375°F. Peel and chop the potatoes into 1-inch chunks. Place in a saucepan and cover with 1½ cups water. Simmer potatoes gently until soft, about 25 minutes, and the water has completely evaporated. Remove from heat, season with salt and pepper, and mash coarsely. Allow potatoes to cool, then mix in the scallion, cheeses, and the egg. Sprinkle in the flour and mix to a uniform, dry consistency, using a small amount of additional flour if needed.

Line a baking sheet with parchment and a generous amount of non-stick pan spray (or 2 teaspoons olive oil). Divide the potato mixture into four equal portions, place them on the sheet, and shape into patties with the back of a well-oiled spoon. Bake for about 45 minutes, flipping the patties halfway through.

Sauté bacon in a large skillet until crisp. Remove the bacon. Pour off most of the bacon fat, add the onion, and sauté until translucent. Add the sliced garlic and sauté 2 minutes. Deglaze the pan with the broth, scraping up any browned bits, then add the kale, currants, and maple syrup. Simmer until wilted and most of the liquid has evaporated, about 8 minutes.

Top potato cakes with the braised kale, garnish with toasted pine nuts and crumbled bacon, and serve with a dollop of sour cream. Serves 4 as a main course, 8 or more as an appetizer. Try them with smoked whitefish or salmon, capers, and fresh dill.

SPICY GREEN BRUSCHETTA

For the spread:

2 oz. fresh herbs in season, chopped coarsely (1½ packed cups)

2 jalapeños (or any hot chile), to taste

1 clove garlic

2 tablespoons olive oil

1 tablespoon tahini

¼ teaspoon curry powder

½ teaspoon liquid aminos, tamari, or soy sauce

½ teaspoon honey

4 oz. cashews, roasted and salted (1 scant cup)

For the bruschetta:

12 to 16 slices baguette

8 oz. halloumi cheese, cut into 12 to 16 slices

Cherry tomatoes, sliced

Preheat the oven to 350°F. Place all of the spread ingredients except the cashews into a food processor and pulse to a coarse, pesto-like consistency. Remove to a bowl, then add the cashews and pulse to a somewhat fine, slightly chunky consistency. Stir the cashews into the herb mixture until fully combined.

Brush the baguette with olive oil and toast in a 350°F oven.

Fry the sliced halloumi in a small amount of olive oil until nicely browned. To serve, top bread with the herb pesto, a slice of the fried cheese, and plenty of fresh tomatoes.

POLENTA LASAGNA

1 lb. ground pork

1 small red onion, cut into small dice (1½ cups diced)

4 cloves garlic, sliced

1 tart apple, peeled and cut into small dice (¾ cup diced)

1 teaspoon ground ancho chile

1 teaspoon ground coriander

½ teaspoon smoked paprika

½ teaspoon granulated onion

½ teaspoon ground mace

¼ teaspoon fennel pollen or ground fennel seed

¼ teaspoon raw sugar (optional)

½ teaspoon liquid aminos, tamari, or soy sauce

¼ teaspoon salt

Pepper to taste

1 lb. butternut squash, peeled

4 oz. shredded Parmesan or aged cheddar cheese

1 cup coarse polenta

4 cups water or broth

1 teaspoon olive oil

½ teaspoon granulated onion

¼ teaspoon salt

Pepper to taste

Using only the neck of the squash, slice into very thin (⅛ inch) rounds. Set aside.

In a heavy-bottomed skillet, sauté the pork, onion, garlic, and apple gently, over medium heat. Heat until nicely browned, about 15 minutes, adding the spices about halfway through the cooking time. Use small amounts of water as needed to deglaze the pan and keep the mixture moist and slightly syrupy. Remove from heat and set aside.

Preheat the oven to 375°F. Cook the polenta in the water or broth along with the olive oil, granulated onion, salt, and pepper, stirring often, until it pulls from the sides of the pan. Grease a 9x9 baking dish. Pour half the polenta into the baking dish and spread evenly with the back of an oiled spoon. Sprinkle half of the cheese over the top, then layer half of the squash slices over the cheese. Next, layer the pork mixture, top with the remaining squash slices, and finally the remaining polenta. Cover with foil and bake for 50 minutes. Remove the foil, top with the remaining cheese, and bake an additional 30 minutes. Allow to set up for 20 minutes before slicing. Serve with plenty of sliced cherry tomatoes or your favorite rustic tomato sauce.

MAPLELAG RESORT

Hope Creamery

"It started with living up north, living off the land, so to speak," explains Jay Richards of Maplelag Resort. His parents, Jim and Mary, relocated with their family to fifty-six acres on Little Sugarbush Lake in 1973. "We actually began with a maple syrup operation." At one time, Mapelag was one of the largest maple syrup producers in Minnesota. "In the peak years, production was almost 500 gallons a year."

Lodging began in 1974, when another maple syrup producer asked to bring a group of friends to rent the loft in their sugarhouse. Jim and Mary saw an excellent way to supplement their sugaring income, so they renovated two small log cabins, and Maplelag Resort was born.

As word of the resort spread, Maplelag expanded, adding new cabins and rooms and attracting the attention of Concordia College of Moorhead, Minnesota. "They thought this would be a great spot for their summer language camp . . . so we built the big lodge." Concordia has leased the site each summer since 1976, flooding the resort with campers for their language immersion programs.

As the resort business grew, the maple syrup production came to a halt. "Now we have 15,000 skiers a year! That's our main business along with the summer language camps." Maplelag has become a premier cross-country ski destination, spreading across 650 undeveloped acres with sixty-four kilometers of groomed ski and bike trails. The rustic accommodations have grown to house up to 200 guests.

Good food is important. "We have high standards for what we serve," Richards says. "People are amazed that we still do everything from scratch; we do not buy any premade, prepackaged food. That's not Mapelag at all." Many ingredients

The Richards family

come from within a few miles of the resort: honey from the Johnson Honey Company in Callaway, wild rice from the nearby White Earth Reservation, and maple syrup from Kroll's in Long Prairie. Jay is especially fond of the butter from Hope Creamery: "We read about them in an article and said, 'Let's try it.' It's fantastic . . . warm, fresh bread out of the oven, served with Hope butter . . . it doesn't get any better!"

Hope Creamery butter is the secret ingredient in Mapelag's Norwegian pancake breakfast, a weekend institution. "If we didn't serve those on Saturday mornings there would be an uprising, a riot!" The pancakes contain more eggs and are thinner than American-style flapjacks but thicker than a crepe. "It's flour, sugar, milk and, of course, lots of Hope butter." Imported

lingonberries, sour cream, and Kroll's pure maple syrup are served for toppings alongside farm sausage and homemade ten-grain hot cereal made with grains from Tochi Foods in Fargo and Meadow Farm Foods in Fergus Falls.

Maplelag's bottomless cookie jars are another guest favorite. "We have five bottomless cookie jars out all the time, 24/7." The jars are kept full with a wide variety of made-from-scratch cookies. "It's just like grabbing a cookie out of grandma's cookie jar. We have chocolate chip, snickerdoodles, ginger cookie, molasses cookie, oatmeal raisin, and monster cookies." Many of the dry ingredients come from Meadow Farm Foods, but it's the Hope butter that really makes the cookies special.

According to Victor Mrotz, owner of Hope Creamery, their butter is unique because "it is vat pasteurized and batch churned. Those two processes are older technology and lend themselves much more to a handmade product. As a result we get a much cleaner product, meaning there are less milk solids in the butter and higher levels of butterfat, which gives a nicer flavor."

Hope butter is well loved by chefs and bakers and can be found widely throughout Minnesota's eateries. Victor says the success of Hope Creamery has grown exponentially with the locally grown food movement: "We were fortunate to get there. We were not the first, but one of the first . . . it has really been a fun ride." The awards and accolades given to Hope Creamery are too numerous to list. Hope has shared this success with other Minnesotan growers and producers as a distributor for local eggs, dairy, and other products. The increasing number of new hands-on, small-batch creameries coming to market is a measure of Hope's trailblazing achievements.

Jay Richards speaks proudly of his relationship with producers such as Hope Creamery. "We like working with other family-run business like ourselves. We're family-owned and operated; we're not a corporation." He feels that his guests notice this difference in their food, even if they may not understand why. "It has a different feel, taste, and experience when you're eating Maplelag food. We get that comment from people. Even more so recently because so much food is mass produced, packaged . . . just heat up and serve. We feel that using as many local people, family-run Minnesotan operations as possible just adds to the eating, dining, . . . culinary experience at Maplelag."

Sourcing this way challenges many businesses, especially those in remote areas. Accessibility can be problematic for the resort; despite being situated in an agriculturally rich region, infrastructure can be lacking aside from the large corporate distributors. "We're making a lot of trips ourselves to get the food. Sometimes we'll have guests that are in these areas and they'll bring things up for us. That's great!" The eight-year relationship with Hope Creamery succeeds in part because the creamery is very well organized for a small producer. "Hope is great . . . we just have to keep track of their delivery days."

Maplelag has a when-we-can-get-it attitude to their sourcing. "We do a pan-fried walleye that I feel is some of the best in the state. It's not deep fried, it's not broiled; it's just lightly fried in oil with our homemade seasoning. I'll put it up against any walleye in the state." When it's available, the walleye comes from nearby Red Lake.

Jay hopes to continue to source locally and sustainably whenever possible, eschewing the markdowns and specials from their food purveyor and giving preference to what small, local producers can provide. "We love food. We like honest food, well prepared and made from scratch. It's a little bit more," he confides, "but we're not looking at best price, we're looking at best quality."

NORWEGIAN PANCAKES

4 eggs

2 cups milk, divided

1 1/2 cups flour

1/4 cup sugar

1/2 teaspoon salt

2 tablespoons melted Hope Creamery butter

Beat the eggs in a large mixing bowl, then add 1 cup of milk. In a separate bowl, whisk the flour, salt, and sugar until well combined. Add to the egg mixture. Beat the batter until smooth, then add the rest of the milk. Stir in the melted Hope Creamery butter just before frying.

Heat a griddle or skillet over medium-high heat and lightly grease with butter. Ladle about 1/4 cup of batter on the griddle and cook until the top just begins to set, about 30 seconds. Turn the pancake and cook the second side until nicely browned. Grease the griddle as needed.

Serve with pure maple syrup, Hope butter, lingonberries, sour cream, farm sausage, and ten-grain hot cereal. Serves 8.

MAPLELAG TEN-GRAIN HOT CEREAL

1 cup rolled oats

1/2 cup rolled wheat

1 tablespoon each rolled barley, bran, rye flakes, cornmeal, cracked brown rice, millet, flax seed, and sesame seeds and/or raw sunflower seeds

Pure vanilla extract (optional)

Salt

Combine grains and store in an airtight container for up to four weeks.

To prepare hot cereal, boil 1 cup of water in a medium saucepan. Once boiling, add about 1/2 cup of hot cereal mixture, a dash of salt, and 1/4 teaspoon of pure vanilla, if desired. Turn down heat and simmer at least 10 minutes until desired consistency, stirring occasionally. For thicker cereal, add more cereal mix, and for runnier cereal, add less. Serve with dash of cinnamon, Hope Creamery butter, Kroll's maple syrup, and/or brown sugar and dried fruit.

MINNESOTA RIVER VALLEY

THE AMBOY COTTAGE CAFE

Whole Grain Milling Company

When Lisa Durkee opened the Amboy Cottage Cafe in 2000, it was a testament to her belief that big things can be done in small places. The cafe is a 750-square-foot renovated Pure Oil gas station, which was built in the 1920s with an English Cottage motif. It seats thirty-one people, if you count the bathroom. Seating does expand in the summer when the gazebo and the outdoor picnic tables are brought out. Nevertheless, reservations are a necessity on weekends.

There are other measures of smallness associated with the cafe. Amboy residents number less than the square footage of their cafe—and it is theirs, Lisa will insist. For the conventional economist, the fact that a cafe in a town of about 600 people is regularly packed at lunchtime is big. That the cafe employs about twenty people part-time in such a tiny town is also big. But there's more to that part of the equation than meets the eye.

"I used to be a nurse in Mankato, a forty-minute commute," Lisa explains. "But I wanted a job close to home. It just made more sense economically and ecologically." Lisa has created a non-commuting job for both herself and other community members.

Lisa Durkee

"A lot of people who work here are related," Lisa says. "We have a number of mother-and-daughter and mother-and-son employee combinations." The cafe also has customer-worker ties. "The daughter of the antique dealer across the street works here," Lisa comments. "Her family walks over and eats here two or three times a day."

Relationship webs like that make economic measurement interesting. It turns out that some of the tables and chairs in the cafe belong to the antique shop and are sold and replaced regularly. "They become more antique-y while they are here," Lisa jokes. "We add value to them."

An antique is a small thing an economist probably can quantify. And economists actually coined the term "value-added." Lisa and her staff often talk about another value-added commodity, what they refer to as the cafe community—the people who bring fresh flowers and garden vegetables to the cafe in the summer and contribute to the paperback book exchange. They also provide the art (for sale!) that hangs on the walls.

How do you measure community? Is it big or small? For one thing, it can fix faucets. "I've got a group of men who come in every morning, and sometimes I barter with them," Lisa says. "I ask them if they'll trade a waffle breakfast in exchange for fixing the faucet." Imagine that the cafe community is part of the "big" side of Lisa's "big things in small places" equation—even if it is a small community.

Is the food "big?" Lisa says it's "slow food"—in contrast to the hectic clip of convenience fare. Those customers who have paced their lives to the beat of drive-by meals may consider the cafe's service to be slow—but it's just a subtle form of encouragement for them to relax and enjoy their meal. "We actually take the time to make a pot roast, and my mom still makes all the pie crusts," Lisa says. "I think the people come for the good food."

When the staff takes the time and patience to make that good food, like the slow-cooked pot roast, hand-rolled focaccia bread topped with olive oil, herbs, and mozzarella, or a hand-rolled pizza crust, they hope the diner will also take the time to enjoy it.

Whenever possible, the Amboy Cottage Cafe uses suppliers who share their notion of good service and "slow food." For example, they serve products from Whole Grain Milling of Welcome, Minnesota. The Hilgendorf family, who own the company, grow organic corn on their farm, which they make into delicious corn chips. The corn chips are favorites with the cafe's homemade chili.

The cafe also serves milk, ice cream, and butter from MOMs, which stands for Minnesota Organic Milk. The vanilla, chocolate, and molasses chip ice cream taste homemade and come from nearby Gibbon. Mike, Diane, and Roger Hartman started MOMs in the 1990s as the first on-farm organic dairy creamery in Minnesota. They felt that small creameries could revitalize the countryside, much like the Amboy Cottage Cafe has helped bring a renaissance to Amboy.

"Small, on-farm creameries can make small dairies like ours profitable," says Mike. "That can create economic opportunities in our small towns, and urban people will be drawn back to the rural areas." Since the Hartmans started their creamery a decade ago, a few more dairies have turned to on-farm bottling and processing, but demand continues to grow faster than the supply. "I wish we could get more MOMs' butter," Lisa says. "People just don't understand how good organic milk and dairy products are."

The crew at the Whole Grain Milling Company

The butter shortage reveals the Hartmans' rejection of the corporate model of "expand or die." MOMs' size meets their needs for income and that's good enough. Lisa accepts that idea implicitly.

Lisa and the Hartmans also agree that there is probably a "right" size for MOMs and the Amboy Cottage Cafe — somewhere in the continuum of small. That way the energy created by their economic activity becomes available, at no cost, to others. That is evident in Amboy, where an art gallery has opened up right next door. "I don't think they would have opened if we hadn't been here," Lisa says. "The cafe brings a lot of people in. I only wish we could get a grocery store now."

Perhaps in time that will happen, but for now Lisa is having fun doing her big thing in her small place. She has no intention of returning to her forty-minute commute and her nursing career. "I think I'm doing more here to contribute to people's health than I was working as a nurse in the modern health care system," she says.

NORTHERN LIGHTS SWISS CHARD QUICHE

Serve hot with baked potato and sour cream, or chilled with a tossed salad. Very pretty!

1 medium onion, coarsely chopped

3 tablespoons butter

1½ cups sliced mushrooms

2 cloves garlic, chopped

1 lb. Swiss chard, cleaned and chopped

4 eggs

1 cup cream

1 cup milk

½ teaspoon salt

¼ teaspoon freshly grated nutmeg, plus more for topping

1 cup grated mild white cheese

1 unbaked pie crust

4 slices Swiss cheese

In a large saucepan, sauté onion in butter for a few minutes. Toss in mushrooms and sauté with onions until soft and beginning to brown. Stir in garlic. Immediately add Swiss chard and steam under a cover for a few minutes until the chard is wilted. Remove from heat.

In a separate bowl, mix eggs, cream, milk, salt, nutmeg, and white cheese. Combine cooked vegetables and egg mixture and pour into unbaked piecrust. Top with 4 slices of Swiss cheese and more grated nutmeg. Bake at 350° until browned and interior temperature has reached 160°.

BUTTERNUT BASIL SOUP

Garnish this aromatic soup with paper-thin red apple slices and freshly snipped purple basil leaves.

Breathe deeply!

1 large butternut squash
1 large onion, finely chopped
2 tablespoons butter
2 tablespoons olive oil
3 cloves garlic, chopped
4 teaspoons dried basil
1 quart well-seasoned vegetable or chicken stock
4 slices American or soft cheese
1 teaspoon balsamic vinegar
Brown sugar, to taste
Salt and pepper, to taste

Scrub the butternut squash and microwave for 3 minutes to soften for cutting. Place on a cutting board and cut in half. Do not remove seeds.

Place the halves, cut side down, on a buttered baking sheet. Bake in a 350° oven until soft. Meanwhile, sauté onion with butter and olive oil in your favorite soup pot until translucent. Add garlic and dried basil. Stir for one minute and enjoy a deep whiff!

Quickly add vegetable or chicken stock and let simmer. When the squash is done, remove seeds and process or mash the pulp until it is smooth, adding a bit of the broth if necessary. Combine the purée with the broth and add sliced cheese. If the soup is too thick because the squash was dry, adjust the texture of the soup by adding more broth. Stir in balsamic vinegar.

Taste the soup and add up to 2 teaspoons of brown sugar to enhance the flavor of the squash. Add salt and pepper to taste.

SEEDED OAT AND POTATO BREAD

Perfect fresh out of the oven with organic butter or toasted for the next day's breakfast!

2 tablespoons yeast
2 cups warm water
1 cup milk
½ cup mashed potato
¼ cup brown sugar or 3 tablespoons honey
1 cup regular rolled oats
3 cups whole wheat flour
¼ cup butter, melted
2 tablespoons sea salt
Bread flour, for kneading
3 tablespoons sesame seeds
2 tablespoons flaxseed
⅓ cup sunflower seeds
Additional melted butter for topping

Soften yeast in warm water and milk. Add mashed potato and brown sugar or honey. Stir in rolled oats and 2 cups whole wheat flour. Let the sponge sit for a few minutes while you melt the ¼ cup butter and gather together your sea salt and bread flour. Turn on the radio to some good music or convince a family member to produce some live rhythms for your kneading accompaniment. Add the melted butter and sea salt. Stir well and add 1 more cup of wheat flour, then switch to adding bread flour until the dough becomes stiff enough to knead. Knead until the dough is smooth and elastic.

Oil a bowl to keep the dough from sticking and rotate the ball of dough until it is coated. Let raise in a warm place for an hour or so. When it has doubled in size, turn it onto a lightly floured countertop and sprinkle sesame seed, flaxseed, and sunflower seeds over the flattened mass. Roll it up and knead it just enough to incorporate all of the seeds. Shape into 2 long loaves, slash tops, and pour a little melted butter over them. Let rest 5 minutes.

Bake at 350°F for about 40 minutes, until they sound hollow when tapped and are nicely browned.

JAVA RIVER CAFE

Dry Weather Creek Farm

It requires a lot of money to get into farming, and many young people do not have a lot of money. The sum of these two facts is that many young people who want to become farmers can't.

There is a solution, however, one that Mark and Wendy Lange of Dry Weather Creek Farm discovered: the Farm Beginnings program. Run by the Land Stewardship Project (LSP), Farm Beginnings offers a series of seminars and workshops for aspiring farmers. It also matches participants with seasoned farmer mentors. Wendy and Mark credit the program for their success. "It really helped us consider our options and set our goals," Wendy says. "Farm Beginnings was the driving force behind our whole operation here, and it was one of the best things we've ever done."

Patrick Moore, one of the presenters for the Farm Beginnings program, is a former LSP staffer from the Montevideo office and the founder of Montevideo's Java River Cafe. When Patrick, along with his family, set up Java River, they insisted that local foods be the focal point of the menu. At the time, Patrick never imagined that he would eventually be able to get locally milled flour for the cafe's homemade breads.

But thanks to Farm Beginnings, and a supportive community, Mark and Wendy now grow grain and mill flour on their farm near Milan. "Our area has a lot of support for our kind of farming and food production," Wendy says. "Patrick has been a

Amanda and Cathy Blaset

great promoter of the local area and the local food system."

The Langes are building their lives as new farmers upon a foundation built by those who have labored before them—not only Patrick and LSP, but by Mark's family, who provided the land. "This farm has been in Mark's family since 1910, but it was not an active farm when we got married in 2001," Wendy says. "Farming was a new venture for both of us. We wanted to bring the farm back to life as naturally as we could, while still making it economically sustainable. I believe that having a diversity of small enterprises that fit together is the right way to go."

The Lange's idea of interlocking diversity has organic certification as its core strength. To be certified organic, a farm must be planted in a diversity of crops. In general, so as to avoid disease and insect infestations, no crop is grown on the same land for more than one year. The Langes rotate crops like flax, wheat, oats, alfalfa, soybeans, and corn over fifty acres. Since their fields are small, they don't grow very much of any one crop. That's how they became flour millers.

"We planted some certified organic crops that first year, but it was really hard to sell them," Wendy says. "Nobody wanted to monkey with 300 bushels of wheat. They wanted a container load or a semi load. I've always had an interest in making flour for bread, but I kind of had a tabletop version in mind!"

Instead of a tabletop grain mill, the Langes discovered a used stone mill in nearby Cottonwood. They bought it, disassembled the cleaner, hopper, scourer, and two stone mills, and reassembled it at their farm. "Putting the mill back together was like doing a big puzzle," Wendy says. "It was originally designed for bakers to make their own flour every day."

Out of their labors, a new product line was born: Dry Weather Creek stone-ground organic whole wheat and unbleached white flour, wheat bran, ground flax, and other products. Patrick helped the Langes place their Dry Weather Creek flour onto the shelves of Bill's Grocery in Montevideo. He also began using it in Java River's baked products.

In late 2005, Patrick left Java River to dedicate his efforts to protecting and restoring water quality and biological integrity in the Upper Minnesota River Valley watershed. Java River's new owners, Cathy Blaset and her daughter Amanda, continue to carry on Patrick's traditions. They not only use Dry Weather Creek flour, but many other products from local farms, as well as beef from their own farm.

"Our cook, Angela, does a wonderful job," Cathy says. "She bakes a different bread every day. The oatmeal honey is to die for. She also makes specialty cheesecakes along with oatmeal scones, muffins, and cinnamon rolls to go with your morning coffee." The soup and bread of the day is the customer favorite. Angela creates a variety of savory soups, including corn chowder, beef noodle, and a stuffed pepper soup. And there's also the Bungalow Burger—made from "a recipe that has been in Montevideo since the 1920s," Cathy adds.

Cathy and Amanda, who manage the daily cafe operations, intend to continue the vision of making Java River more than just a nice cafe. "It's more of a gathering place," Cathy says. "People come and sit and talk. It's like a little haven. I hope that when people walk in the door they feel welcome and comfortable."

Cathy and Amanda are committed to nurturing local artists as well as local farmers. Java River's engagement with the arts, Cathy says, was one of the primary reasons she chose to purchase the cafe. "I'm an artist myself, and I know it's a hard way to make a living," she says. "If I can encourage people to purchase from local artists, that's great. There is a lot of talent in the area. We change the art on the walls monthly, with one show in the front and one in the fireside room." People also come to Java River to use the upstairs meeting room, an extension of the concept of the cafe as a public house.

Java River's stated goal "is to stimulate the rebirth of a new economy based on locally produced, quality foods, and creative cultural expression." Because one cafe alone may not be able to create the climate for that rebirth, the formula for that bold vision is made up of many variables. But those who are hungry for a taste of an emerging new economy can do so by enjoying bread and soup, and joining the conversation at Java River Cafe in Montevideo.

Serving up breakfast at the Java River Cafe

Wendy and Mark Lange

COUNTRY WHOLE WHEAT BREAD

If you like to bake bread, you'll love putting both of these loaves together. The dough is a baker's dream, and so tasty.

Makes 2 loaves

Proof in large mixing bowl:
1 tablespoon yeast
1½ cups warm water
¼ cup powdered milk
⅙ cup shortening
¼ cup brown sugar, packed

Mix in separate bowl:
⅙ cup ground flax
1½ cups organic whole wheat flour
½ tablespoon salt
2 to 2½ cups unbleached white flour

Proof the yeast by dissolving it in a warm liquid (sometimes with a small amount of sugar) and setting it aside in a warm place for 5 to 10 minutes until it swells and becomes bubbly. This technique proves that the yeast is alive and active and therefore capable of leavening a bread or other baked goods.

Add flour and flax mixture to the proofed mix and knead until dough is smooth, about 8 minutes. Cover and let rise in a warm place 30 to 40 minutes, and then form two loaves. Place the loaves in two 8½x4-inch greased pans. Cover and let rise an additional 30 minutes in a warm location.

Bake 35 minutes at 350°F or until loaves are golden brown and sound hollow when tapped.

CRANBERRY MULTI-GRAIN BREAD

Makes 2 round loaves

Proof in large mixing bowl:
1 tablespoon yeast
1½ cups warm water
¼ cup powdered milk
⅙ cup shortening
¼ cup brown sugar, packed

Mix in separate bowl:
⅙ cup ground flax
½ cup organic whole wheat flour
1 cup oatmeal
½ tablespoon salt
1 cup dried cranberries
2 to 2½ cups unbleached white flour

Add flour and flax mixture to the proofed mix and knead 8 to 10 minutes. Cover and place in a warm spot, let rise 30 to

40 minutes, then form into two round loaves. Put parchment paper on a cookie sheet and sprinkle cornmeal on the parchment; set loaves on the cookie sheet. Let rise 30 more minutes. Bake 35 minutes at 350°F or until loaves are golden brown and sound hollow when tapped.

Note: A sprinkle of coarse kosher salt on the top of the loaves before baking adds a nice contrast to the cranberries.

SAINT PETER FOOD CO-OP

Shepherd's Way Farms

Shyma O'Brien was born and raised in Saint Peter, Minnesota, but if a stranger asks him where he grew up, he won't think twice about his answer. "I grew up in the co-op," Shyma says. The "co-op" is the Saint Peter Food Co-op in the small Minnesota town of the same name.

"I've been working in the co-op for sixteen years," Shyma, now in his late twenties, says. Since Shyma's mother, Margo, has been the general manager of the cooperative since its inception, and since co-ops of the 1980s tended toward non-hierarchical work organization, it's easy to imagine a fourteen-year-old Shyma stocking shelves. When he was in his late teens, Shyma began working in the deli. Now he oversees it.

The deli offers fifty to seventy-five items, including twelve varieties of pre-made sandwiches a day. Along with the sandwiches are an array of salads—pasta, rice, fruit, and vegetable. "We have pre-pack entrees too," says Shyma, "like spinach mushroom lasagna, Creole roasted yams, and spanikopita—a spinach pie with layered filo dough, feta cheese, and lots of herbs."

The menu changes with the seasons to take advantage of fresh, local produce. "In late summer, we'll have tomato and mozzarella salad, because that's when tomatoes are in season," explains Shyma. "We get locally grown cherry tomatoes, heirloom tomatoes and fresh basil. We mix them with olive oil, salt and pepper, add fresh mozzarella, and it's fantastic."

Shyma O'Brien

Other seasonal favorites are tomato basil soup with feta and velvety yam soup with fresh dill and cream.

Shyma's strategy has been to provide foods familiar to rural and small town Minnesotans, along with more adventuresome and ethnic foods. The deli also features a range of artisanal foods from area producers. Among these are an assortment of cheeses, including five varieties of Eichten's Gouda from Center City, Stickney Hill's goat chevre from Kimball, various cheeses from Bass Lake in Wisconsin, and queso fresco, Friesago, and Big Woods Blue from Shepherd's Way Farms near Nerstrand.

Shyma knows most of the local cheese suppliers as well as many of the other vendors personally. "We are committed to supporting local sustainable agriculture," he says. But just what "committed" means took on a whole new dimension when Shepherd's Way Farms, owned by Jodi Ohlsen Read and Steven Read, experienced a devastating tragedy a couple years ago.

A few hours before dawn on a frigid January morning in 2005, the Read family was awakened by their neighbor. "He told us our barn was on fire," Jodi says. "We can't see that part of the farm from our house and by the time he called, things were pretty bad. We went out and tried to get the sheep out of the barn, but it was difficult."

The fire brought out not only the local fire department, but the neighborhood. Despite the efforts of the family, neighbors, and firefighters, the fire killed 200 lambs and 300 ewes and destroyed all of the farm's housing for sheep. The loss was not just economical, but deeply emotional. But when Steve gathered his family together later that morning and asked if anybody wanted to quit, the resounding answer was "no."

There have been times that family members have wavered since that predawn commitment. And the farm has yet to recover economically. It will be, Jodi says, a long time before the negative economic impact of the fire is no longer felt. But Jodi, Steven, and their children have persevered. They continue to shepherd and milk their sheep, and Jodi continues to make award-winning cheeses. They do this not only because of their personal will but because their community of employees, neighbors, and customers stood by them in a manner that was a testimony to their vision on how food should nurture people.

"When you have a tragedy like that it's not surprising that your family and your friends, and maybe your neighborhood and town, come and help you out and bring casseroles," Jodi says. "It's what people do. But after the fire, we understood we were part of a much bigger community. I hadn't realized how tightly knit we all are until this happened, and the co-ops and stores and restaurant owners and people who use our food came out with the most amazing support I've ever seen in my life.

"They were at our door with wonderful meals for us and our volunteers. People volunteered their time. People who had never spent any time with animals were out there helping put ointment on the sheep's burns. The co-ops took contributions from customers and helped sustain the farm. Without that kind of outpouring we wouldn't be here today." The Saint Peter Food Co-op was part of this community—providing food for volunteers and holding a fundraiser for the farm.

"One of the things people talk about a lot now is that people more and more want to know where their food comes from," says Jodi. "That can sound trite. It can sound like a marketing gimmick. But now I know it's real. People want to know the stories of the people who are responsible for their food. They want to feel connected to those people. It really showed in the response to our fire."

It was because of the support of that wide circle of friends and customers, as well as their family, that Jodi and Steven decided to take their cheeses to the American Cheese Society conference in Louisville, Kentucky, that same year. There they received four awards: their Friesago, Hope Queso Fresco Garlic Herb, Hope Queso Fresco, and Shepherd's Ricotta all received awards.

If you, by chance, find yourself carrying your tray to the spacious and sunlit seating area of the Saint Peter Food Co-op's deli, and if you have a salad with Big Woods Blue or a sandwich with Shepherd's Hope Queso Fresco, do savor the complex award-winning flavors. And know, that by nourishing yourself with that cheese, you are also savoring a wide and strong net made from threads of strong, brave, and triumphant lives.

Saint Peter Food Co-op and Deli

The Read boys: Aidan, age 15; Elia, 12; Maitias, 9; and Isaiah, 10

79

VELVETY YAM SOUP

A wonderfully velvety soup made with yams.
Serves 6–8

Olive oil for sautéing
2 leeks, chopped, use only white and light green
4 large sweet potatoes, peeled and sliced
1 tablespoon vegetable beef broth powder
2½ cups water
2 teaspoons dry dill weed
1⅓ cups heavy cream
1⅓ cups half & half
½ teaspoon each sea salt, black pepper, white pepper; adjust
  as needed

In a medium stockpot, sauté leeks in a small amount of olive oil. When leeks are tender, add the peeled and sliced yams, vegetable broth powder, water, and dill weed and simmer until all are tender.

Purée in a food processor (or blender) with the heavy cream and half & half. Heat gently in a large stock pot until warm.

Season with sea salt, black pepper, and white pepper, and serve.

Olivia gathers ripe heirloom tomatoes

CAPRESE SALAD

Use only the best quality, freshest ingredients available in this salad. A variety of heirloom tomatoes would create a feast for your eyes—Green Zebra, Homestead, Lemon Drop, Russian Black, Brandywine. A drizzle of aged balsamic vinegar would provide a sweet finish.
Serves 2–4

4 large homegrown tomatoes, sliced
1 lb. fresh mozzarella, sliced
6 fresh basil leaves, cut as chiffonade*
1 tablespoon extra virgin olive oil
Fresh cracked pepper
Sea salt

On a tray, layer a tomato slice and then a fresh mozzarella slice. Repeat this process until the tray is full. You can start in the middle and work your way out in a spiral pattern or arrange in multiple straight lines.

Top tomatoes and fresh mozzarella with fresh basil. Drizzle with olive oil and sprinkle with black pepper and sea salt.

*To chiffonade, stack leaves, rolling them tightly, then cut across the rolled leaves with a sharp knife, producing fine ribbons.

Opposite page
Upper right: Steven Read and Jodi Ohlsen Read
Bottom: Steven Read in the meadow with his flock

BLUFF COUNTRY

NOSH RESTAURANT & BAR

Rochester Farmers Market

reg Jaworski likes to shop at the farmers' market. On any given Saturday morning during market season, Greg and some of his staff will meet at 6 AM at the kitchen at Nosh, his restaurant in Lake City. "That way we can be downtown at the Rochester market when it opens at seven," Greg says.

Seeing, touching, and smelling the freshly harvested ingredients they will use at the restaurant is a passion for the Nosh chefs. "I've told my crew that I can't pay them while we're at the market," says Greg, who has been seen burying his nose lovingly into a fresh head of fennel. "They come anyway."

Greg and his staff stroll through the Saturday Rochester market and Wednesday's Lake City market, visiting both their favorite farmers and anyone who has enticing produce. "I like working with the farmers who get excited about the things they raise, like the first carrot of the year," Greg notes.

The Nosh crew knows they'll probably find asparagus and rhubarb in the May markets and carrots in the September markets. There is a rhythm. There are also surprises and unanticipated early arrivals. For instance, the pregnant question about the arrival of the first sweet corn is conceived sometime

Greg Jaworski

around the delivery of the first tomato and the discovery of a flat of glowing golden raspberries among a dozen simmering reds.

There are times when Greg wishes Nosh was a little further down the Mississippi so he could gain some weeks of growing season. The seasonal rhythms would be more languid; less abrupt. As it is, Nosh has adopted some traditional strategies to compensate.

"We've learned to preserve things," Greg says. "I use morels we've dried in spring, and we do a lot of freezing. We'll buy a few extra flats of raspberries at the peak of the season and freeze them. We also put up strawberries."

The frozen strawberries are used in a recipe that conjures up memories of grandmothers, back porches, and summertime. "We'll have a fresh rhubarb coffee cake when we're using the last of our frozen strawberries to make ice cream," Greg says. "We use local cream and eggs for the ice cream. We'll use goat's milk to make fresh cheeses like queso blanco and queso fresco."

Nosh also turns local pork into house-made sausage. Made-in-restaurant mustard, such as cherry mustard and apricot mustard, is another house specialty. To go to the farmers' market and return to prepare mustard, ice cream, and queso blanco, and then put up raspberries, requires more kitchen time than most restaurants are prepared to give. On Saturdays, the Nosh staff is back from the market and in the kitchen by 10:30 AM.

"It's definitely more work," Greg says. "It's a difficult industry as it is. The hours are extremely long, and when we spend an additional five to ten hours a week going out in the field to find ingredients, it makes for a long week."

One of the great challenges for any restaurant is to find farmers who are prepared to sell products directly. "Several months before the restaurant opened, I spent a lot of time going out and visiting farms," Greg says. "All the terminology, like organic and free range, isn't that important to me; I wanted to see for myself how they run their business and to talk to them."

The staff at Nosh will probably never put aside their ardor for rubbing elbows with the people who grow their ingredients. However, plenty of other restaurants are unable to dedicate staff time to shopping the markets. These establishments find the Southeast Minnesota Food Network, a for-profit distribution web, to be a constructive alternative.

"We have about forty restaurant and retail accounts," says Pam Benike, a dairy farmer, artisan cheesemaker, and coordinator for the Southeast Minnesota Food Network. "We have ninety members who produce a large variety of food—everything from meat to vegetables to cheese to freshly made pies. We can provide one source for marketing, distribution and invoicing services for our members, saving farmers a lot of time and expense."

The Southeast Minnesota Food Network arose out of a need: small farms have to compete with the large warehouses and distribution chains that large restaurant supply and grocery corporations use. That need has been affirmed by university research and think tanks in the Upper Midwest.

Residents in southeast Minnesota spent about $500 million buying food from outside the region between 1997 and 2003, according to Ken Meter of the Crossroads Resource Center. Ironically, Ken's research has shown that farmers spent about the same amount buying inputs—everything from fertilizer to baling twine—from outside southeast Minnesota. If consumers and farmers were to look closer to home for their needs, southeast Minnesota's small towns would likely experience a renaissance in the next decade or so.

There are different strategies for remaking agriculture and rural communities in southeast Minnesota. The Southeast Minnesota Food Network's collaborative distribution is one such strategy. Vibrant farmers' markets are another. The ultimate strategy for eaters, whether dining at home or at a restaurant like Nosh, is to increasingly insist on high-quality, regionally produced food.

"I feel that it's truly the way a restaurant should be," Greg says. "What our farmers are growing, or what I can find at the market, is what I can put on the menu. It's much fresher, and our customers are very happy to be supportive of local farms."

GRILLED BERKSHIRE PORK LOIN WITH TWO-POTATO
HASH AND ELDERBERRY DEMI GLACE

Grill a seasoned pork chop or loin approximately 4 to 6 minutes on each side, or until internal temperature reaches 140°F. (Cook times can vary greatly due to grill temperature differences and thickness of the cuts.)

Allow to rest for a couple of minutes before serving with Two-Potato Hash and Elderberry Demi Glace.

TWO-POTATO HASH
Serves 6

½ lb. bacon, small diced

3 large Yukon Gold potatoes, medium diced

2 large sweet potatoes, medium diced

1 medium sweet onion, medium diced

1 red bell pepper, small diced

1 tablespoon garlic, minced

1 tablespoon chili powder

1 teaspoon ground cumin

1 tablespoon minced fresh Italian parsley

Salt and pepper to taste

Preheat oven to 400°F. Render bacon in large sauté pan over low heat until just crispy, about 10 minutes. Remove bacon with slotted spoon and reserve. Add potatoes and onion to the bacon fat, season with spices, salt, and pepper, and sweat the vegetables for 5 minutes. Stir constantly to avoid sticking to the pan and to evenly coat vegetables with the fat and seasonings. Transfer to sheet pan and roast until the potatoes are just cooked through, about 20 minutes. Add bacon, just to reheat. Taste and check for seasoning.

ELDERBERRY DEMI GLACE
If you're unable to find elderberries, substitute blackberries or raspberries.

1 quart elderberries, cleaned and removed from stems

¼ cup sugar

3 cups good-quality beef stock

1 teaspoon kosher salt

½ teaspoon freshly ground pepper

1 tablespoon butter

Salt and pepper to taste

Cook elderberries in a small saucepan over low heat with sugar until sugar dissolves and berries wilt and burst, approximately 15 minutes. Strain through a fine mesh strainer to extract as much juice as possible while removing seeds and skins. Return the elderberry juice to pan with the beef stock and reduce the liquid to sauce consistency, about 1½ cups. Remove from heat, season with salt and pepper, and whisk in butter until it is incorporated.

GRILLED LAMB CHOPS WITH BLUE CHEESE BREAD PUDDING AND TOMATO-CUCUMBER RELISH

Season 8 to 10 lamb (or goat) chops generously with salt and pepper. Grill on each side for four minutes, or until chops reach an internal temperature of 105°F for medium-rare.

BLUE CHEESE BREAD PUDDING
Serves 6–8

1 day-old baguette, diced
6 eggs
1 quart milk
1 pint heavy cream
4 cups crumbled blue cheese
1 sweet onion
2 tablespoons minced garlic
2 tablespoons chopped parsley
Salt and pepper to taste

Preheat oven to 375°F. In a heavy-bottomed saucepan, sweat the onion and garlic in butter until soft. Add the milk and heavy cream, season with salt and pepper, and bring to a boil. Remove from heat. Place the diced baguette in a large bowl, pour the cream mixture over the bread, and stir until well mixed. Let stand for about a half an hour for the bread to absorb the milk mixture.

In a small bowl, whisk the eggs and fold into the bread mixture. Fold in the cheese and parsley. Pour into a greased 9x11-inch baking pan and cover with foil.

Bake for approximately 40 minutes, then uncover and continue to bake until golden brown on top, about 15 minutes more.

TOMATO-CUCUMBER RELISH
If using cherry tomatoes, simply halve them.
Yield: 4 cups

1 pint good-quality tomatoes, different varieties if possible, diced large
1 large cucumber, or 2 small cucumbers, seeded and diced
1 lemon, juiced and zested
1 tablespoon minced fresh mint and basil
2 tablespoon extra-virgin olive oil
Salt and pepper to taste

In a bowl, add all ingredients and allow to marinate.

ROASTED BEET SALAD

This is a Nosh favorite!

6 medium beets, roots and tops trimmed
Olive oil to coat
½ cup pecans, chopped and toasted
⅓ cup high-quality blue cheese, crumbled

DRESSING
1 cup balsamic vinegar, reduced to ⅓ cup
½ teaspoon red pepper flakes
½ teaspoon ground cinnamon
½ teaspoon allspice
⅛ teaspoon cayenne

Preheat oven to 425°F. Toss beets in olive oil to coat. Place beets on a sheet tray and roast until tender (approximately 35 to 45 minutes), let cool.

Prepare dressing. Toast pecans.

When cooled, peel and cut beets into wedges. Put 4 to 5 wedges on a plate and sprinkle the pecans and blue cheese on top. Drizzle the reduced vinegar over the top. Wilted greens add nice color and flavor. This salad can be made up to a day in advance.

LINZER TART

11 oz. unsalted butter, softened

10 oz. sugar

2 eggs

1½ teaspoons cocoa powder

1 teaspoon ground cinnamon

½ teaspoon ground cloves

8 oz. cake flour

11 oz. finely ground hazelnuts

1 oz. cake flour

2 teaspoons lemon zest

10 oz. high-quality raspberry preserves

Cream the butter and sugar until light and fluffy. Add the eggs one at a time, not adding the second egg until the first egg is incorporated. Sift together the cocoa powder, the first measurement of flour, and spices. Add the ground hazelnuts and zest to the flour mixture, then add to the creamed butter and mix until just incorporated. Weigh out 18 oz. of the dough and mix in the second amount of the flour. Reserve this dough at room temperature.

Place the remaining dough (without the added flour) in a pastry bag with a small plain tip and pipe out the dough over an 11-inch tart pan, starting at the outside edge, making concentric circles to evenly cover the pan. Try to use all the dough to achieve the correct thickness of crust.

Bake at 375°F for about 15 minutes or until the crust just starts to color. Remove from oven and cool slightly. Spread the preserves evenly over the crust, leaving a 1/4-inch border around the outside.

Place the remaining dough in the pastry bag with the same tip. Pipe straight parallel lines, about a half inch apart, across the tart. Then pipe a second set of lines across the tart at a 45 degree angle to the first set.

Bake again at 375°F for about 25 minutes, or until there is a nice golden brown color on top; check frequently. Cool the tart before eating.

This tart will actually benefit by being made up to a day ahead for best flavor and results, since the nuts in the dough will absorb moisture from the air and most importantly the jam, making for a moist pastry.

DANCING WINDS
FARMSTAY RETREAT

Callister Farm

"When we get close to going to market, it's like getting ready for a performance," says Lori Callister, a farmer from the Northfield area who is a vendor at the Midtown Global Market with her husband, Allen. "I get really pumped up. Where else in the world can you get a job where people tell you they need your product so badly? If I didn't have that customer contact, I don't think I could continue. It's like an elixir."

Mary Doerr, proprietor of Dancing Winds Farmstay Retreat, is a neighbor to the Callisters. "I use to make artisan goat-cheese," says Mary, "but cheesemaking was a little isolating for me. One of the reasons I was able to transition out of cheesemaking is because the farmstay was growing. I really enjoy the social aspect of it, and creating a safe haven for people. I also like to expose people to goats. I guess that's ultimately my mission."

Mary and Lori's agricultural projects emerged from a long history of neighboring during a time of immense creativity and change in southern Minnesota's agricultural scene. Mary's vision, which continues to evolve, was born from the flames of tragedy.

"I started milking goats in September of 1985," Mary recalls, "but I had a barn fire a year and a half into it and lost the barn and a lot of the goats." But the fire sparked her inspiration for building the cheese plant, which eventually transformed into her bed and breakfast venture.

Mary Doerr

Among those who were there to provide Mary fortitude, as she gathered up the ashes of her barn and charred goats, was Ken Taylor. Mary remembers how Ken was himself a guiding light to her and so many others as he forged the now widely shared vision of an inextricable link between urban and rural people.

During the early 1980s, while Ken Taylor was creating the Minnesota Food Association, a coalition of urban and rural citizens working towards a sustainable food system, the Land Stewardship Project and Nature Conservancy were bringing together some of the best and brightest farmers of southeastern Minnesota to form the Sustainable Farming Association. It was within that farmer-driven organization that Lori and Mary first collaborated.

"We were both on the board of directors of the Sustainable Farming Association's Cannon River Chapter," Lori remembers. "When our family first joined, about 1990, it was because we were committed to raising crops and poultry without chemicals and antibiotics."

"It was fun because we had creative people like Dave and Florence Minar, Dan and Muriel French, Mary Doerr, and Mike and Linda Noble," Lori says, recalling some of the pioneers in Minnesota's movement toward a new agriculture. "We were very active with field days and learning from each other. There

were a lot of interesting things going on."

The Minars and Frenches led the way in grass-fed dairying. The Minars now run Cedar Summit, one of the premier on-farm dairies in the country where they make outstanding milk, cream, yogurt, and ice cream. The Frenches are part of a small cooperative that produces the nationally award-winning Pastureland butter. The Nobles are leaders in direct-marketing sustainably produced pork, chicken, and more recently, lamb.

Mary and Lori have blazed their own trails as well, but like the others, continue to collaborate. A few years ago, when Lori was

Lori Calister

still making her own handcrafted jams and jellies, Mary served the jeweled creations to her bed and breakfast guests. Today, Mary gets her preserves from Mary Ellen Frame, another Sustainable Farming Association contact. And since the Callisters have become full-time chicken, turkey, and egg producers, Mary's guests also enjoy the Callisters' poultry products. Mary doesn't cook breakfast for her guests, rather she stocks the refrigerator in her farmstay with fine local ingredients that guests can use to make their own meals.

"I get a lovely seasoned chicken sausage from the Callisters," Mary says. "My guests who are meat eaters love that." The Callister family makes a wide range of sausages, which come in bulk, links, and patties, from their chickens.

"I use all my own recipes," Lori says. "We make an herb sausage, an Italian sausage and an apple-maple sausage, using local apples and maple syrup. We get the syrup at the Saint Paul Farmers' Market from Mark Christopher, who is from Spring Valley, Wisconsin. We get cranberries for our cranberry sausage from another Wisconsin farmer at the market. It started out as a turkey sausage because I wanted something that tasted like Thanksgiving dinner, and it evolved to chicken. We also have a savory mushroom and wild rice sausage. We get our wild rice at the farmers' market, as well."

Mary doesn't participate in sausage production on the Callister farm, but every Wednesday, in exchange for fresh poultry, she helps butcher and package chickens. But Mary doesn't go to butchering day just to earn a few drumsticks.

"It takes ten or twelve of us to process poultry," Lori says. "At noon, we have a big meal together. It's a nice social hour for everybody, mostly neighbors and friends. Even when we butcher, there's a lot of socializing."

As part of this extended community, Mary earns not only chicken and eggs, but bragging rights. When she stocks her guests' refrigerator and cupboards with food from the Callisters, Frenches, or Mary Ellen Frame, she's likely to share stories that go along with the food.

"I want to promote the sustainable farmers who are nearby," says Mary. "I want to promote the good products that people are making and raising. And while it allows me to be on a soapbox a little about sustainable agriculture, I'm very careful not to jam anything down their throats. I'm a bit more subversive; I believe I can get to them through their stomachs.

"It's really fun to be able to say, 'this butter is from grass-fed cows,' and the reason it's so marvelous is because those cows are on fresh grass getting lots of exercise and sunshine."

In fact, Mary's entire farmstay experience, modeled after European-style farmstays, is pretty low key. Guests can cook and eat according to their own schedule and rhythm. They can sleep in or get up early and go bird watching. They can walk the meditation maze that Mary maintains. They can help with chores or milk a goat—or they can just commune with the goats.

"Goats are incredibly affectionate animals," Mary says. "They are friendly, lively and, like a cat, demand affection on their own terms. They are also comical. They'll come up to the fence and want their ears scratched. In the summer I welcome people to put plastic over their boots and just sit in the pens with the animals. Some of my favorite guests come at least for a couple of the seasons. The husband enjoys bird watching while his wife relaxes in the barn, where the goats form a line to get brushed."

Knowing that people take that kind of pleasure in her beloved goats is an elixir for Mary, just like visiting with customers at the Midtown Global Market is a tonic for Lori Callister.

CHEVON MEAT LOAF

Serves 6

2 lbs. ground chevon (goat meat)
1 cup tomato juice
1 small onion, finely diced
1 carrot, diced
2 eggs
1½ cups dried breadcrumbs
1 teaspoon dried sage
Salt and pepper to taste

Mix all ingredients together. This should be a bit moist as chevon is a very lean meat. Turn the mixture into a greased loaf pan. Cook at 400°F 1 to 1½ hours, or until a knife comes out clean. You can add a ketchup glaze on top of the loaf during the last 15 minutes. Serve with candied yams.

ASPARAGUS WITH GOAT CHEESE AND MORELS ON FETTUCCINE

Serves 4–6

½ cup shallots, minced
2 tablespoons unsalted butter
½ cup dry white wine
½ cup chicken broth
½ lb. fresh morels or other brown mushrooms, such as porcini, sliced crosswise
½ cup heavy cream
8 oz. mild goat cheese (about 1 cup)
¾ lb. asparagus, trimmed, cut into ½-inch pieces, cooked in boiling salted water for 2 to 3 minutes, or until tender, but still bright green
¼ cup fresh chives, minced
¾ lb. fettuccine

In a heavy skillet, cook the shallots in butter over moderately low heat, stirring until softened; add wine and simmer the mixture until the wine is reduced by half. Add the broth and the morels and simmer the mixture, covered, for 10 minutes or until the morels are tender. Add the cream and the goat cheese and cook the mixture over low heat, stirring until the cheese is melted. Stir in the asparagus, chives, and salt and pepper to taste. Keep the sauce warm.

In a kettle of boiling water, cook the fettuccine until it is *al dente*. Drain it well, and toss the pasta with the sauce in a bowl.

HERB GOAT CHEESE QUESADILLAS

Serves 8

1 lb. chevre (fresh goat cheese)
½ cup low-fat milk
1 tablespoon fresh basil, chopped
1 tablespoon fresh cilantro, chopped
1 tablespoon fresh parsley, chopped
1 tablespoon fresh sage, chopped
8 flour tortillas
½ cup olive oil

Preheat oven to 375°F. Combine goat cheese and milk in a bowl. Mix together and add the fresh herbs. Spread ¼ cup cheese mixture onto each flour tortilla and fold in half. Brush tortillas with olive oil and place on a baking sheet. Bake for 8 to 10 minutes or until golden brown. Cut each in half and serve warm.

CALLISTER'S BEER CAN CHICKEN

1 farm-fresh chicken, ¾ to 1 lb. per person
1 teaspoon granulated garlic
1 teaspoon paprika
1 teaspoon cinnamon
1 teaspoon black pepper
1 teaspoon oregano
1 teaspoon sage
1 teaspoon sea salt
1 teaspoon onion powder
½ can beer

Mix spices together and rub mixture on outside of chicken. If you have a roasting stand for the chicken, use it. It holds the bird upright and allows the juices to drip down into the pan. Place the pan in the oven or on the grill first. Pour beer into the bottom of the cooking pan. Place the chicken into the pan. Bake for about 20 minutes per pound at 375°F. Juices will run clear when done. A thermometer placed in the thigh of the chicken should read 180°F. You can also pour the beer directly into the cavity, if desired.

PEOPLE'S FOOD CO-OP

Dream Acres Farm

*I*n 2011, members of Rochester's Good Food Store cooperative voted to merge with People's Food Co-op of nearby La Crosse, Wisconsin. "Then our members stepped up and invested a million dollars to make this project happen," says Brad Smith, Member Services Manager. The larger co-op now operates out of two locations, one in La Crosse and the other in a new 15,500-square-foot store in downtown Rochester. "About half of those members were from La Crosse. Most of those shoppers will never shop at the Rochester store more than once or twice but they were still willing to make that investment." That's a strong showing of support for the merger and the co-op mentality.

The Good Food Store in Rochester dates back to 1975, when a group of organizers, meeting at the public library, founded the store. Modest at first, with a focus on natural bulk goods, the grocery grew in popularity as it overcame the challenges of a new member-owned style of operation. The co-op was dealt a blow during a severe 1978 flood, which wiped out the store and inventory. In spite of the early setback, members rallied and the store was rebuilt, operating successfully until the 2011 merger.

Before the co-op's relocation, downtown Rochester had been designated "Food Insecure" by the USDA. This was a short step away from "Food Desert," which describes severe lack of access to fresh, healthy food. City officials and developers

People's Food Co-op

were motivated to correct the problem, and they sought out partners to build a new grocery store. According to Brad, the Good Food Store was approached about an expansion, but the co-op's board of directors felt they had insufficient resources. While membership was loyal and supportive, their ranks were small, numbering less than 1,000. "So the board approached the La Crosse co-op's board and asked if they would be interested in partnering, saying we can make this happen if we share resources," says Brad. A few votes later, the members of both co-ops declared their approval, and the Good Food Store was slated to relocate downtown, rebranded as People's Food Co-op.

Membership in Rochester has increased rapidly since the merger, more than doubling in the first year. The new space features more room for organic and local produce, the addition of fresh seafood and local meats, a coffee and tea bar, and an expanded deli. Brad wants to make sure that the changes are welcomed and embraced by the longtime co-op members. "We're sort of walking this tightrope of making sure that we carry on the tradition of the Good Food Store, which our members have come to expect, but also reintroducing ourselves to the city of Rochester." It's a balancing act they must constantly consider.

The People's Food Co-op carries forward its predecessors' legacy in its deli. Though for efficiency and synergy they have merged the deli menus in both locations, they have preserved favorites from the Rochester Co-op. "Two of the things we feature that were Rochester recipes are our Awesome Wraps and our Oat Pecan Burger," says Deli Manager Maura Henn. The Oat Pecan Burger is a savory vegetarian burger patty flavored with basil and sage; the Awesome Wrap features marinated tofu with cajun seasoning and sautéed vegetables stuffed into an whole-wheat wrap. They're very popular with current members and can be ordered up fresh from the deli staff.

Maura has helped expand the offerings to meet the demand of busy downtown eaters. Members can enjoy a wide, changing menu with choices such as Shrimp in Coconut Rice, Moroccan Couscous, Garlicky Cassoulet, Pad Thai, and more.

Maura began working with the People's Food Co-op's La Crosse store in 2004. There she also managed a local farmers' market, bringing local farmer and producer connections back to the store. This is something she hopes to continue in Rochester, where the new location neighbors the local market. "It's just so satisfying to be able to bring in local produce and work with local vendors," says Maura, who enjoys building relationships producers and their families. "You can really see the connectedness of the food." One farm with deep connections to the co-op is DreamAcres of Wykoff, Minnesota.

With their two sons, Todd and Eva run a small subscription vegetable business in a beautiful basin about thirty-five miles from Rochester. The farmstead is off the grid, and the family relies solely on solar, animal, and human power to run their home and livelihood. They till their fields with oxen, making the already pastoral setting seem even more so.

Less of a typical vegetable farm, DreamAcres is more a multifaceted approach to rural homesteading. Beyond growing vegetables, Todd and Eva host a variety of events throughout the year. Each Friday throughout the summer is pizza night, where the family serves up organic wood-fired pizza with toppings fresh from the fields. They also host workshops on their farm, adding to the curriculum of local schools and colleges as well as teaching private courses. Timber framing, maple sugaring, blacksmithing, draft animals, and solar energy are among the class offerings.

Eva, a founding member of the Looking Glass Theater in Chicago, is an active artist and brings her passion and expertise to special summer programming at the farm. Flourish is a week-long summer camp for children, linking performing arts, dance, music, theater, puppetry, and agriculture in a total-emersion educational experience. Eva also coordinates master-class arts retreats, live theater, and music performances in the DreamAcres Barn, which is set up as an art and performance space. To help manage the programs, Eva and Todd founded the Dreameary Rural Arts Initiative, a nonprofit organization.

Todd and Eva are also pound members of People's Food Co-op. "They are our closest and best source of organic items that we don't grow on the farms," says Todd. "We get our sugar and flour for the pizza nights there." Todd works with Bulk Department Manager Dave Lawsone to special order the pantry items for their various functions. "We really rely on the staff," he says.

Brad Smith envisions a growing number of relationships, such as the one with DreamAcres, in the store's future: "What makes us functional is the health and well-being of our local farmers, but for us to support them we need our consumers to also search out and support their products."

Serves 4–6

This simple yet tasty version of the popular dish can be made with ingredients easily found at your local food co-op.

Dressing:
$^1/_4$ cup lime juice
$^1/_2$ cup soy sauce or tamari
$^1/_2$ cup ketchup
2 tablespoons brown sugar

8 oz. wide rice noodles
2 tablespoons peanut oil
1 tablespoon minced ginger
2 tablespoons minced garlic
1 teaspoon crushed red pepper flakes
1 small jalapeño pepper, seeded and minced
16 oz. firm tofu-cubed, $^1/_2$ inch dice

2 cups shredded carrots
1 can bamboo shoots, drained
$^1/_2$ cup cilantro, chopped
1 cups green onions, sliced diagonally, $^1/_4$-inch thick
1 cup peanuts, roasted

Whisk dressing ingredients together, then set aside. Cook rice noodles according to the instructions on the box, then drain and rinse with cold water to prevent overcooking—a slightly al dente noodle is best. Heat peanut oil in a wok or large, wide-bottom pan over medium heat. When hot, add garlic, ginger, red pepper flakes, and jalapeño. Sauté until fragrant, about 15 to 30 seconds. Add tofu and cook evenly on all sides. Add carrots and bamboo shoots and cook gently until carrots are tender. Add dressing, heat to a light simmer. Carefully add the cooked noodles and heat until warm. Gently fold in cilantro, green onions, and peanuts until well combined.

SCANDINAVIAN INN

Hilltop Pastures Family Farm

The Scandinavian Inn and the Hilltop Pastures Family Farm suit each other well. "We met Peter Torkelson at a Lanesboro Chamber of Commerce meeting," Sara Austin, of Hilltop Pastures, says. "Peter said he might be interested in some of our eggs and pork products and invited us to come by for a visit. My husband and I are committed to building local relationships and selling our food directly to our customers."

That kind of thinking has a strong appeal to Peter Torkelson, who runs the Scandinavian Inn with his wife, Vicki, and is a retired employee of the Minnesota Pollution Control Agency. Peter prefers a lifestyle that allows him to walk and bicycle, rather than drive.

"My goal is to have the inn make as small of an ecological footprint as possible," he says. "We call ourselves an environmentally sensitive bed and breakfast. That means we buy locally as much as we can and serve organic produce when we can. We use natural cleaning products and soaps. We use no synthetic chemicals or fertilizers on our lawn, mow with a back-powered reel mower and clear our sidewalk with a shovel."

Peter and Vicki have been innkeepers since 2004. During that time, they have developed a sense of what an environmentally sensitive inn is. Although Peter says the concept is evolving, part of it is simply living in a town where he and his

Peter Torkelson

guests can walk the few blocks to Lanesboro's picturesque downtown. Some of the other practices they've put into place include providing cloth napkins at breakfast, brewing shade-grown, fair trade coffees, line-drying towels and linens outdoors when the weather permits, and buying local and organic foods.

So when Peter had the opportunity to serve Sara and Tom Austin's eggs in a porta-bello mushroom dish, he was more than happy to do so. He was particularly charmed that the shells came in three colors: blue, brown, and white.

Sara, who left her job at the Mayo Clinic in 2004 to raise a family and, along with her husband Tom, become a farmer, is excited for the opportunity to fill that gap for the Torkelsons and others near her farm.

The philosophies of the Austin and Torkelson families align in terms of being environmentally sensitive in how they run their respective businesses. The Austins have adopted a system written about extensively by Virginia farmer, Joel Salatin, that rotates cattle, pigs, and chickens on pastures. It is a "beyond organic" system that maximizes the health of the animals, grasses, and soil.

If you visit the farm, you will see pigs happily rooting in the mud, cows grazing on rolling pastures, and chickens pecking away at the grass in their portable pens. "When the grass is green, the chickens are always outside," says Sara. "They love it."

The Scandinavian Inn is just one of the bed and breakfasts in town that have this commitment to buying locally grown foods. Down the street at the Cady Hayes House, Peggy Hanson will also serve you farm-fresh eggs and vegetables from her husband Frank's garden. And if your timing is right, you may also get morels or other wild foods that Frank has foraged from the woods around Lanesboro.

In fact, the commitment to local foods ripples throughout this small community of less than a thousand people. Up the road at the Eagle Bluff Environmental Learning Center, community members and visitors can come to "Dinner on the Bluff," the first Saturday of most months. Here guests partake in a delicious gourmet meal made with local ingredients, followed by a presentation from a noted speaker.

So come to town to bike or ski the miles of trails, canoe down the Root River, or shop in the charming stores. Pick up a Green Routes brochure and explore unique and interesting places in the area. Stay at the Scandinavian Inn, Cady Hayes House, or one of the other bed and breakfasts in town. And ask about the stories behind the food you are being served.

Tom and Sara Austin and their children Shane, Sami, and Caleb

Breakfast at the Scandinavian Inn

NORWEGIAN ROMMEGROT CREAM PUDDING

Serves 6–8

½ pound butter (2 sticks or 1 cup)*
½ cup white flour**
1 quart half & half***
2 tablespoons sugar
½ teaspoon salt (or slightly less)

Melt butter (reserve ¼ cup) in a large pan. Lightly sauté flour in the butter over medium-low heat. At the same time, heat half & half in saucepan over medium-low heat until it is shiny on top or until scalding. Scalding temperature is 150°F. If a skin develops on top of the cream, remove it before proceeding.

Add hot half & half slowly to flour and butter mixture, stirring constantly. Never reverse direction. (I use a flat whisk because I prepare the butter-flour mixture in a large sauté pan.) Add sugar and salt once all half & half has been incorporated. Keep stirring until the Rommegrot comes to a boil. Pour Rommegrot into a heat-safe bowl, or pour into a crock pot set on low.

To serve, pour reserved ¼ cup of melted butter on top and serve Rommegrot warm. This approximates the traditional method of preparing and serving Rommegrot. At the Scandinavian Inn we often serve the Rommegrot at room temperature, with no melted butter on top and sprinkled with cinnamon and sugar.

Note: I have had success dividing this recipe in half and even in fourths.

* If you don't wish to serve Rommegrot with the reserved ¼ cup butter on top, begin with only ¾ cup (1½ sticks) of butter.
** Since my usual organic white flour is a little bit heavier than commercial flours, I often take out 1 teaspoon or so of flour so the pudding will not get too thick.
*** Equal parts of milk and heavy (whipping) cream can be substituted for half & half.

DANISH RØDGRØD RASPBERRY PUDDING

Serves 4

½ lb. fresh raspberries
About 1½ cups water
2½ tablespoons cornstarch
6½ tablespoons sugar
½ tablespoon lemon juice
Pinch of salt
Whipped cream

In a medium saucepan, combine berries and water. Bring to a boil, simmer for 5 minutes. Strain out seeds and save liquid. (I first force them through a colander or other coarse strainer, then through a fine strainer, then through a cloth.) Discard seeds. Add enough water to make 2 cups of liquid and return to the saucepan. Add lemon juice.

Combine dry ingredients in a measuring cup or small bowl, stirring thoroughly to blend cornstarch and sugar. Slowly add spoonfuls of the liquid and stir until a thin paste results.

Bring liquid to 185°F or a very low simmer, and pour the paste into the liquid, stirring constantly with a wire whisk. Maintain the temperature and stir with whisk for about 5 minutes until thickened to a jelly-like consistency. Cover and cool for a few minutes. Pour into 4 sherbet glasses. (If pudding has skinned over, stir with whisk before transferring to sherbet glasses.) Refrigerate.

Serve cold with a dollop of whipped cream on top.

VEGETARIAN QUICHE

Serves 8

PIE CRUST

1 cup whole wheat flour (we use pastry flour)

⅓ cup cold butter

3 to 5 tablespoons cold water

In a mixing bowl, cut cold butter into flour until pea-sized balls are formed. Add water, one tablespoon at a time, until dough is moistened and workable. Roll dough or press into a 9-inch glass pie pan to form the bottom crust.

Liz says, "I tend to have difficulty getting all of the dough evenly moistened. After I have removed and pressed into place the workable part of the dough, I tend to add more water to the drier flour that remains in the bowl. I usually make the pie crust while the cooked vegetables are cooling."

QUICHE FILLING

5 eggs

1 cup milk

2 cups cheese, shredded; use a mix (we typically use equal amounts of mild cheddar, sharp cheddar, and Monterey Jack)

1 large onion, chopped

1 small-to-medium head of broccoli

1 cup sliced mushrooms

About 1 to 2 tablespoons dried tomatoes, broken into small pieces

Cooking oil

1 teaspoon dried rosemary

1 teaspoon dried sage

½ teaspoon dried parsley

½ teaspoon dried leaf marjoram

½ teaspoon dried basil

¼ teaspoon black pepper

Peel and coarsely chop onion. Cut up broccoli (head and stem) into about ¾-inch pieces. Drain mushrooms.

Measure out herbs into a coffee cup or other small bowl. (Fresh herbs can be used as available. We typically use chopped fresh basil, sage, and parsley from our garden but usually add some dried sage with the fresh. Use about three times the amount of fresh to dry herb.)

In a large frying pan, fry onions for about one minute in oil, add mushrooms and continue to fry until onions begin to brown, then add chopped broccoli and cover for one minute. Uncover, stir in herbs and continue to fry for 30 seconds. Remove from heat and add dried tomato pieces. (We usually freeze the dried tomatoes, then remove them from the freezer and quickly crush them with our hands while they are still frozen and brittle.) Cool.

Sprinkle a layer of shredded cheese in the pie shell. Remove the broccoli heads from the frying pan and evenly spread those over the cheese. (Do this to ensure that the broccoli flowers are buried within the quiche. If they are on the top and exposed to the heat, they will burn.) Sprinkle some of the remaining vegetable mix onto this layer. Add a layer of cheese, a layer of vegetables, a layer of cheese, and finish with a layer of vegetables on the top.

Add milk and eggs in a bowl, and mix. At this point you can pour the egg/milk mixture into a covered container, cover the quiche, and refrigerate both overnight. Combine them the following morning just prior to baking. Pour eggs and milk into pie shell.

Baked uncovered in a 350°F preheated oven for 75 minutes. Remove from oven and allow to stand for 5 to 10 minutes before serving.

TWIN CITIES AREA

RESTAURANT ALMA AND BRASA

Otter Creek Growers

"What I'm doing isn't a trend," says Alex Roberts, owner of Restaurant Alma. "At least as far as I'm concerned it's not. The only way I know how to cook is with seasonal foods. I prefer local ingredients if available because local farmers produce the best food. If the level of quality puts me in a higher price range, I'm OK with that. I grew up with food from the garden, good whole foods, and that's what I serve."

Working with food that's as fresh as possible and controlling it in its natural state is the way Alex works. No par-baked bread or mixes. "Society is very accepting of processed food, and in fact, they trust food that's in a package. Somehow it's 'cleaner' because it's packaged and has a pretty label. The perception is that a local farm can't provide that level of safety, and it's just not true," Alex says. "Others think that 'food is food.' Just because you can eat it, doesn't mean it's food."

Some of Alex's favorite customers are those in their seventies and eighties. "They'll come in and say, 'This is the way I remember food tasting when I was a kid,'" he explains. "That's because that food came right off the farm or from the garden just like the food we use here."

As a hands-on restaurateur—and father of young children— Alex doesn't travel much these days. But he does credit his time in New York and Florence for providing a good base for what he does. In those places, he learned to work with fresh ingredients and with constantly changing menus.

Alex Roberts

At Restaurant Alma, Alex likes to have a mix of the old and the new on his menu. "When I'm developing a menu, I look at what's available," he says. "Since my dad farms, I know when specific crops are at their peak and I structure my menu from there. We always have red meat, white meat, fish, shellfish, and vegetarian choices on the menu, so there's enough variety for everyone." Even if crab is on the menu, you can feel comfortable that it was a "good" purchase. Alex will only buy seafood caught using sustainable practices and from areas that aren't overfished.

"I've worked with many of the same suppliers for years," Alex comments. "Dave and Florence Minar of Cedar Summit Farm provide me with exceptional dairy products. My dad's stuff (Otter Creek Growers) is on par with anyone's. I don't bounce around a lot. My suppliers are planning on my order and I stick with them."

Alex's new restaurant in northeast Minneapolis, Brasa, is less upscale than Restaurant Alma but includes many of the same seasonal, local ingredients. Here, he focuses on more universal foods—rotisserie chicken, slow-roasted pork, red beans and rice, corn, braised greens, grits, and sweet potatoes. "Food is the best medicine," Alex says. "It's the things you have to include in your diet, not what you need to avoid, that is important. That's the way it has been for most of the history on this planet. I like to think what I'm doing is normal."

FENNEL GRATIN

3 cups fennel bulb, sliced
1½ cups leeks, white part only, sliced
1 cup sweet onion, diced small
Zest of one orange
2 cups fennel cream (recipe below)
1½ cups coarse-grated Parmesan cheese

Mix together fennel, leeks, and onion with salt and pepper. Place half of the vegetable mixture in a lightly greased 9x13-inch pan. Top with half of the Parmesan cheese and orange zest. Top with remaining leek and fennel mixture. Pour the fennel cream to almost cover vegetables, and top with other half of cheese. Cover with foil and bake at 350°F to 375°F until vegetables soften, about 25 minutes. Uncover and bake until lightly browned.

FENNEL CREAM

2½ cups cream
1 piece star anise
1 tablespoon fennel seed
½ yellow onion, rough chopped
Salt and white pepper to taste

Combine ingredients and simmer until reduced to 2 cups.

SWEET CORN FLAN

Serves 6
3 cups fresh corn kernels
Butter, for sautéing
Toasted and ground cumin, salt, tumeric, and white pepper, to taste, for seasoning
½ cup cream
7 egg yolks
Truffle oil, for seasoning
Pinch of tumeric

Sauté the corn gently with a nub of butter, cumin, white pepper, salt, and a pinch of tumeric; remove from heat when softened. When corn has cooled, blend with cream, yolks, and truffle oil. Strain this mixture through a fine chinois and pour into prepared molds (8 oz. ramekins) coated with non-stick spray. Bake in a water bath at 350°F for 40 to 50 minutes or until just set.

SEASONAL GREENS SOUFFLE

Serves 12

2 lbs. fresh chard
¼ cup unsalted butter
¼ cup reconstituted porcini mushrooms, chopped
¼ cup fontina cheese, or mild-flavored melting cheese, diced
2½ cups bechamel sauce (recipe below)
3 eggs, separated
Salt and pepper

Cook greens, in just the water clinging to the leaves after washing, for 5 minutes. Drain, squeezing out as much water as possible, and chop. Gently sauté the greens in butter for 5 to 7 more minutes; remove from heat. Allow to cool, then stir the greens, porcini, and fontina into the bechamel sauce, then stir in egg yolks one at a time. Beat the egg whites until stiff peaks form. Gently fold in beaten egg whites into cheese sauce. Pour mixture into prepared molds (8 oz. ramekins). Bake in a water bath of simmering water at 350°F for 30 to 40 minutes, or until set.

BECHAMEL SAUCE

¼ cup butter
¼ cup all-purpose flour
2 cups whole milk
Salt and pepper
Pinch of nutmeg

Melt the butter in a pan over medium heat, whisk in the flour until incorporated, then add milk, whisking constantly until it comes to a boil. Season with salt, lower the heat, and cover and simmer gently, stirring occassionally for at least 20 minutes. Remove from heat; adjust seasoning with pepper, nutmeg, and more salt if needed.

BRYANT LAKE BOWL, BARBETTE, AND RED STAG

Moonstone Farm

Rewards come in many different ways. It doesn't get much better than when you're able to act on a desire to make a difference and actually see it happen. When Kim Bartmann opened Bryant Lake Bowl (BLB) in 1993, she set forth to create a venue with a relaxed atmosphere, affordable prices, and good food. This funky restaurant/bar meets bowling alley meets cabaret theater became a quick success in the Uptown neighborhood.

But a few years ago, Kim had a crisis of conscious with her job. She says, "I already had a strong value system for providing healthy food, but I wanted to align some of those healthy food values with better environmental practices." Inspired by a Business Alliance for Local Living Economies conference she attended, Kim set out to be more environmentally responsible in her restaurants.

"First off, I made the decision to get as much sustainably and locally grown food as possible for our menu," Kim says. "This means less fuel is used in transporting food, the land is better cared for by those using sustainable farming practices, and more money stays in the local community." With the opening of Barbette in 2001 and the Red Stag in 2007, Kim is able to expand her impact in the community and on the landscape.

Kim only hires chefs who share her mindset. "I've hired a forager to strengthen and seek out partnerships with additional growers. There's a need to know what a grower can consistently

Kim Bartmann

get for us, and how quickly they can ramp-up for additional needs or ventures," Kim says. "We also need to look at how new products can be worked into our menu."

Beyond buying food from local farmers, Kim also is committed to educating others. BLB highlights a different producer each month on their menu, and customers gets to "meet the farm and the face" behind the food. For instance, they might meet Audrey Arner and Richard Handeen from Moonstone Farm in Montevideo, who provide the grass-fed beef for the burgers at BLB. The steaks she gets from them are featured on the menu at Barbette. Audrey and Richard are part of Pride of the Prairie, a network for local, sustainable farmers in western Minnesota.

At the Red Stag, Kim has gone a few steps further. The building is the first LEED-certified restaurant in the state, meaning it incorporates green technologies into its design and operation. Kim also has a van that will pick up products from smaller farms. And this won't be just any van, it will run on vegetable oil from the restaurant fryers. Good for the environment, good for the farmers, good for BLB, Barbette, and Red Stag.

Kim says, "Yes, we are preaching to our customers, but most of them want to know where their food comes from. While the idea of local or organic is still a bit of a barrier for some people, we overcome that."

Audrey Arner and Richard Handeen

CHICKEN WINGS IN BARBECUE SAUCE

This barbeque sauce is used on BLB's organic, free-range chicken wings from Larry Schultz Farms. BLB roasts the chicken wings ahead on a cookie sheet at 375°F for about an hour. When ordered, they are grilled and then tossed in a pan with the sauce. Deliciously spicy and so good with the Black River Blue Cheese Dressing (below).

Yields about 5½ cups

1½ cups brown sugar
½ cup butter
¾ cup white vinegar
1 cup ketchup

One 5-oz. bottle Heinz 57 sauce
1 tablespoon whole celery seed
1 cup diced yellow onion
¼ cup Sriracha chili sauce (this garlic hot sauce can be found at many large grocery stores or Asian markets)
1 tablespoon lemon juice

In a saucepan, caramelize butter and sugar on medium heat until bubbly. Add vinegar and whisk until lumps are gone. Add all the other ingredients and simmer on low heat until thickened. Cool and refrigerate in an airtight container. Holds for about one week.

DIJON MUSTARD VINAIGRETTE

BLB serves this dressing on its Star Prairie (Rainbow Springs) smoked trout and beet salad.

Yields about 3¼ cups

½ cup Grey Poupon Dijon mustard
2 tablespoons champagne vinegar
1 cup fresh lemon juice
2 tablespoons dried thyme
½ teaspoon kosher salt
½ teaspoon cafe coarse-ground black pepper
1 cup extra virgin olive oil
½ cup honey

Mix mustard, vinegar, lemon juice, thyme, salt, and pepper in a food processor or a bowl. Slowly add olive oil to create an emulsion while running food processor or whisking continuously. Then slowly add honey in the same way.

Put in airtight container and store in the refrigerator. Holds about one week.

BLACK RIVER BLUE CHEESE DRESSING

The Black River Blue Cheese from Wisconsin is perfect in this dressing, tangy yet mild enough for those who don't like blue cheese. This will become your favorite dressing, as a dip or on a salad. BLB also uses this dressing on its organic grilled bison salad (Silver Bison Ranch) and on its organic grass-fed mushroom and blue cheese burger (Moonstone Farm).

Yields about 2 cups

1 teaspoon minced garlic
⅓ teaspoon (or to taste) ground black pepper
⅔ teaspoon (or to taste) white pepper
⅓ teaspoon (or to taste) dry ground mustard

1 tablespoon white wine vinegar
⅓ cup plain yogurt
⅓ cup sour cream
⅓ cup mayonnaise
2⅓ tablespoons buttermilk
⅔ cup blue cheese crumbles
4 tablespoons minced parsley

Mix all ingredients well in a bowl. Store in airtight container in the refrigerator. Holds for about one week.

MENDOBERRI CAFÉ & WINE BAR

Thousand Hills Cattle Company

When dining out in Twin Cities suburbs, there are plenty of choices as long you don't mind eating at the chain du jour. Amid the cookie-cutter concepts with their tired commercial fare, a unique and charming cafe has quietly been dishing up an alternative. Chef/owner Robert Ulrich of Mendoberri Café & Wine Bar struggled to find places to take his family where he felt comfortable with what they were eating. "It's a very repetitive system," he says. "We were always finding the same processed foods." He and his wife, Ann, began planning their restaurant, hoping, "There must be more people out there who think and feel like we do."

They opened the Mendoberri Café in October 2010 with a vision to bring farm-to-table, from-scratch foods to a neighborhood where this notion had been largely unavailable. "It definitely was a risk," he says. "In a sense we're pioneers here." Fortunately, he had struck a chord with his Mendota Heights neighbors, who've come out in droves. "They always tell me we give them what they've wanted; they don't need to go far away to search for a restaurant with quality food, nice ingredients . . . locally sourced." For suburban dwellers, a chef-driven, farm-to-table concept is a refreshing delight.

Robert Ulrich

The restaurant splits its day to better serve its guests. Daytime hours feature a quick-service style; busy eaters can step up to the counter to order a scratch-cooked, wholesome meal, served in house or packaged to go. At 4 p.m., Mendoberri goes full service, inviting diners to linger in the airy dining room. The space stuns with its modern open kitchen and prominent furnishings, including a large fireplace, cascading waterfall, and Ann's impressive handmade cork mosaic. Families are welcomed, and Robert and Ann created a children's play area complete with a fully stocked toy kitchen near the front of the restaurant.

An award-winning international chef, Robert began his culinary apprenticeship at fifteen with the Intercontinental Hotels Group in his childhood hometown of Vienna, Austria. His globe-spanning resume traces its zigzag path through four-star hotels, premier cruise lines, and boutique fine-dining concepts. In the mid-1990s, he was promoted to executive chef of the Marquette Hotel, in Minneapolis, a fine accomplishment at twenty-six years of age. It was during his six-year span at the hotel that he met Ann, a Minnesota native. The two married and shortly thereafter relocated to the East Coast.

Years later, after the birth of their first child, the couple moved back to Minnesota to be closer to Ann's parents. Robert spent the first year fleshing out the Mendoberri concept. Deeming farm-to-table an essential component, he began looking for farmers to partner with. "I knocked on doors and told them my concept. . . . I didn't have any money in my pocket, just an idea in my head. The first farmer who responded positively was Lisa Klein from Hidden Stream Farm and she's still one of my main go to farmers." It grew from there. "I got to know more people and people go to know me. I had folks come in, saying I'm growing tomatoes in the summer." Another strong relationship developed with the Thousand Hills Cattle Company, which supplies their grass-fed beef.

"We love it, it's a great product," says Robert. "They believe in what they do . . . we feel very proud to say where the beef is from, just thirty miles away." Based in Canon Falls, Minnesota, Thousand Hills represents a network of independent family farms, which strictly follow their producer protocols. Farmers must employ good pasture and grazing management, including fencing, watering systems, and flexible, rotational grazing. They must pay close attention to the grass and endeavor to improve the quality and quantity of forage available to the cattle. Genetics are crucial, as certain breeds fare better at pasture.

"The British breeds do best on grass," says Todd Churchill, founder of Thousand Hills. "The Continental breeds take too long to mature. If you buy grass-fed beef in France, it's from three- or four-year-old animals. The meat is tough and requires special cooking."

Grass-fed proponents have a list of reasons why raising cattle on grass is favorable. Among these is research that indicates that grass-fed beef is healthier because it has higher amounts of the beneficial omega-3 fatty acids.

Robert serves up Thousand Hills Beef in his Swedish Meatloaf Sandwich, burgers, and entrée specials. His menu is influenced by the daily harvests of his farmers, with nods to his Austrian heritage in his Apple Strudel and ever-changing Schmankerl Board. German for *treat* or *delicacy*, the appetizer pairs house charcuterie and other savories with homemade jams and relishes. You might find a rich liver and apple mousse, prepared by Sous Chef Ryan Olufson, served with an onion jam or chutney. The components reflect the ingredients at hand, in this case, lamb freshly delivered by Lisa Klein.

For Chef Robert, it's important to know his product is safe, wholesome, and something he can stand behind. He says diners have become more and more concerned about the sourcing and safety of the food they eat. When they ask him questions, he says, "I can easily answer in an honest way . . . it is a more natural food, has been treated well, processed in a good way." And that's an answer you can stomach.

Todd Churchill

SWEDISH MEATLOAF

Served at Mendoberri Café on artisan bread with tomato jam, Fontina cheese, crisp bacon, sliced tomato, and fresh lettuce.

1 lb. Thousand Hills ground beef
2 eggs, beaten
3 oz. heavy cream
1 teaspoon Worcestershire sauce
1 tablespoon Dijon
3 tablespoons ketchup
1 fresh shallot, diced
4 oz. bread crumbs
1 tablespoon fresh chopped thyme
1 tablespoon fresh chopped rosemary
1 tablespoon fresh minced garlic
Sea salt and white ground pepper to taste

Preheat oven to 350°F. Combine all ingredients and mix well. Form the meat mixture into a log shape and place on parchment paper lined sheet or roasting pan. Bake in the oven for about one hour, or until the internal temperature has reached 165°F. Let rest for 10 to 15 minutes before slicing, or cool immediately in refrigerator for later use.

TOMATO JAM

8 oz. fresh peeled whole tomatoes

1 bay leaf

3 tablespoons red wine vinegar

1 cup brown sugar

$^1/_2$ teaspoon onion powder

1 teaspoon ground black pepper

$^1/_2$ cinnamon stick

Combine all ingredients in a non-reactive saucepan and bring to simmer. Cook and stir frequently until the liquid has reduced by half. Remove the cinnamon stick and blend in a blender or food processer with a couple of quick pulses to a puree. Strain and refrigerate for later use.

APPLE STRUDEL

DOUGH

2 cups all-purpose flour

$^1/_2$ teaspoon salt

1 large egg

Lukewarm water

1$^1/_2$ tablespoons vegetable oil

Melted butter, for brushing

Combine all ingredients and work into soft and elastic dough. Knead the dough until releases from your hands and the table. Shape the dough into a ball, brush with oil, and let it rest for at least 20 to 30 minutes. On a floured cloth, roll out the dough into a rectangular shape. With the back of your hands, continue to stretch the dough out until it is very thin and almost see-through. Brush with melted butter.

BUTTERBROESEL (roasted bread crumbs)

$^3/_4$ cup bread crumbs

4 tablespoons butter

Melt the butter in a pan, add bread crumbs, and stir until the crumbs are golden brown. Set aside.

ZIMTZUCKER (cinnamon sugar)

$^3/_4$ cup caster/superfine sugar

1 tablespoon ground cinnamon

Combine cinnamon and sugar. Set aside.

FILLING

1 recipe *butterbroesel*

1 recipe *zimtzucker*

1 cup raisins

2 teaspoons fresh lemon juice

2 teaspoons rum (Austrian Stroh Rum is best)

2$^1/_4$ lb. Granny Smith apples peeled, seeds removed, sliced

Preheat the oven to 375°F. To assemble the strudel, sprinkle the filling onto the stretched dough. Cut off and remove the thick edges. Using the floured cloth, roll the dough into a strudel (log shape). Brush melted butter onto the strudel and bake for 45 minutes to 1 hour, until golden brown.

BIRCHWOOD CAFE

Riverbend Farm

Birchwood Cafe owner Tracy Singleton explains it this way: "We're not just *in* the neighborhood, we're *for* the neighborhood."

That neighborhood is the Seward area of Minneapolis, where it's easy to concur with the cafe's website description of what you'll find: "A crossroads of hot food and cool comfort, Birchwood Cafe is one part funky coffee house, one part neighborhood cafe, and two parts eclectic organic kitchen." The cafe's motto is "Good Real Food," and everything on the menu typifies this slogan in the most creative way.

Before opening Birchwood, Tracy waited tables at Lucia's—owned by Lucia Watson, one of the region's best-known local-foods advocates. When she opened her own restaurant, Tracy was able to continue to work with many of the same local vendors. For Tracy, the rewards come not only from serving good food, but from supporting small, local farmers who are critical to a healthy food system.

A hefty amount of the produce on Birchwood's menu comes from Greg Reynolds at Riverbend Farm in Delano. Whether discussing the upcoming crops, paging through seed catalogs, or on a field trip at the farm picking beans and radishes, Tracy and her staff garner a lot of inspiration from this relationship. "Each season Greg asks, 'What can I grow for

Tracy Singleton

you?'" Tracy says. "And my thought is always, how can I best showcase his beautiful food?"

Tracy truly values the personal nature of these relationships. It is the part of her job she loves most. "I really appreciate the opportunity to chat with my farmers and producers. They are the face of our food. Victor Mrotz from Hope Creamery, Pat Ebnet from Wild Acres, and the Hilgendorf family from Whole Grain Milling, we all face similar challenges of running a small business according to our values," Tracy says. She loves the summer deliveries, these hard-working farmers with their children in tow, happy to be helping out. "I always send them off with a cookie or lemonade or a loaf of rye bread made with the flour specially milled to our bread baker's specifications," she says. These relationships are at the core of Birchwood Cafe's "good real food."

When Tracy bought out her former business partner in 2004, the internal reorganization that was required gently forced her into thinking about what she was doing and why, and helped to solidify her mission and values. "At heart, the Birchwood Cafe is about connectedness and relationships," she says. "Basically, we are building community through food. We live in such a fragmented world. Cooking with local seasonal ingredients helps ground and connect us to the earth. This lends a sense of respect for the ingredients we use and an appreciation for the food we eat which connects us to each other and our community."

Tracy likes being the connection point for her customers and farmers. She says, "When you have that connection with a sense of place, and you know where your food comes from, I think we're all better for that."

Greg Reynolds

ROASTED PUMPKIN HAND PIE

Birchwood uses Riverbend Farm's Cinderella pumpkin or sunshine squash, as well as cipollini onions, when available. They choose aged goat cheese from Mount Sterling, Wisconsin.

Serves 8 as a main course; 12 to 16 as an appetizer

FILLING
1 medium sweet pumpkin or butternut squash
¾ lb. aged goat cheese, coarsely grated
2 lb. cipollini onion, roasted
¾ cup olive oil
¾ cup white wine
4 bay leaves
2 sprigs fresh thyme
2 tablespoons peppercorns
Salt and pepper, for seasoning

Cut pumpkin into wedges. Oil and season; roast in 350°F oven just until cooked through, about 45 minutes. In roasting pan, mix onions with olive oil, white wine, bay leaf, fresh thyme, and peppercorns; cover with foil and roast 15 to 20 minutes in

375°F oven. Mix cheese with onions and pumpkin. Season mixture with salt and pepper. Set aside, prepare dough for crust.

CRUST
8 oz. cream cheese
1 cup unsalted butter, Hope Creamery preferred
½ tablespoon salt
2 cups flour

The butter makes all the difference in this pastry, which is why Birchwood always uses Hope Creamery unsalted butter. Beat butter and cream cheese until combined. Add flour and salt and mix until a smooth dough ball is formed. Cut into 6 equal pieces and roll into balls. Using a rolling pin on a floured surface, roll out dough to make about an 8-inch circle. (Make smaller circles if you are making this as an appetizer portion.) Scoop filling onto the middle and fold edges up over the filling. Brush with cream and cook in 375°F oven for 20 to 30 minutes, or until golden brown.

This is served at Birchwood with a simple watercress and Granny Smith apple salad, tossed in a light champagne vinaigrette.

FARRO CARROT CAKES WITH FENNEL KUMQUAT PISTACHIO SALAD AND CARROT COULIS

Farro is the ancient Italian grain from which all others derive. It is similar to spelt but with a firm chewy texture. The success of French farmers supplying the grain to elegant restaurants has sparked renewed interest in farro. Choose packaged farro carefully to make certain you are getting *Triticum dicoccum* (farro's Latin name).

6 cups farro; or wheat berries or spelt
3 cups cannellini beans or other white beans
2 tablespoons olive oil
1 bulb garlic
3 cups shredded organic carrots
3 oz. flour
$\frac{1}{2}$ tablespoon cumin
$\frac{1}{2}$ tablespoon ground ginger
$\frac{1}{2}$ tablespoon salt
$\frac{1}{4}$ tablespoon pepper
2 tablespoons lemon juice

Rinse farro and cook until tender, about 30 minutes. Use 3 parts water to 1 part grain. Check every ten minutes to avoid overcooking. The farro should not split open. This is a sign that you have overcooked the grains.

Cook cannellini beans, or other white beans, and cool. Using a food processor or food mill, purée to a smooth, light consistency with extra virgin olive oil and garlic. Shred carrots to finest consistency with a food processor or box grater. Combine grains, bean mixture, carrots, and remaining ingredients and mix thoroughly.

Fry on griddle till just browned. Serve with Fennel Kumquat Pistachio Salad and Carrot Coulis (recipes below).

Farro Carrot Cakes can be made up to two days in advance and kept refrigerated. Reheat in oven to serve.

FENNEL KUMQUAT PISTACHIO SALAD
2 bulbs fennel, shaved or thin julienne
6 kumquats
$\frac{3}{4}$ cup toasted pistachios
Red wine vinegar
Olive oil
Salt and pepper to taste

Combine shaved or julienned fennel, thinly sliced kumquats, and toasted pistachios in a bowl. Drizzle lightly with vinegar (you can always add more, but you can't take away), olive oil, salt, and pepper. Toss lightly, and arrange on the plate.

CARROT COULIS
3 medium-sized carrots, peeled and uniformly diced
1 small yellow onion, julienned
1 clove garlic
4 basil leaves
3 cups vegetable stock
Salt and pepper to taste

In a small saucepan, lightly sauté carrots, onion, and garlic until onions are transparent. Use low heat and do not caramelize the vegetables. Add basil, and cover with vegetable stock. Simmer for 3 to 4 minutes, remove from heat and purée in a blender. Adjust taste with salt, pepper, and a small dollop of extra virgin olive oil. Serve sauce at room temperature.

STRAWBERRY RHUBARB COBBLER

Delicious served with a drizzle of Cedar Summit cream or a scoop of ice cream. Birchwood uses seasonal strawberries through Footjoy Farm or Southeast Minnesota Food Network; rhubarb through Riverbend Farm, when in season; cornmeal from Whole Grain Milling, Welcome, Minnesota; and unsalted butter from Hope Creamery.

Serves 8–10

FILLING

3 pints strawberries, quartered
2¼ lb. rhubarb, cut into ½-inch pieces
3 tablespoons cornstarch
1½ cups sugar
½ teaspoon cinnamon
1 big pinch nutmeg

Toss fruit into cornstarch, sugar, cinnamon, and nutmeg. Pour into 9x13-inch greased pan. Bake at 400°F for 40 to 50 minutes, or until fruit is bubbly around the edges and juices are thickened and clear. Prepare topping while fruit is baking.

TOPPING

1½ cups flour
½ cup yellow ground cornmeal
½ cup sugar
1 tablespoon baking powder
¼ teaspoon salt
6 tablespoons cold, unsalted butter, cut in pieces
¾ cup heavy cream

Combine dry ingredients. Add butter and cut in until the mixture has the consistency of coarse sand. Gradually add cream until dough pulls together. Break off pieces and spread evenly over fruit. Return to oven and bake for 25 to 30 minutes until golden brown.

CORNER TABLE

Stone's Throw Urban Farm

"It was very organic," Chef Thomas Boemer says, as he explains how he came to partner with Nick and Chenny Rancone after Scott Pampuch's departure from Corner Table a couple of years ago. Under Pampuch, the small south Minneapolis restaurant was a leader among advocates for local eating. With Boemer behind the counter, things are a bit more subtle. He explains, "We're not as vocal. We work with farmers and try to speak through our food. When people come to our restaurant and eat the food, that's the pulpit for us."

In the years since that transition, the number of local farmers hoping to sell their produce has swelled, as has the number of restaurants in the neighborhood. Thomas realized he had to focus on aspects of the food system and community that he thought were most important. That's where Stone's Throw

Thomas Boemer and Nick Rancone

Stone's Throw Urban Farm

This intersection of pragmatism and idealism growing in Corner Table's neighborhood appealed to Thomas, as did Stone's Throw's beautiful produce.

According to Thomas, the most successful way to get people beyond the ignorance most of us have about where our food comes is to "put a plate in front of them with something on it that they've never seen before—or a way of using a simple vegetable that they've never thought of," to get them to start asking questions. He has intrigued diners with the simplicity of their chioggia beet carpaccio, for example. "We start with chioggia beets because they're so incredibly beautiful. We slice them paper thin on a meat slicer we use just for vegetables. Then we macerate the beets in vinaigrette. It just takes a few minutes. When you taste it, it's very light, sweet and herbaceous. Many people have come

Urban Farm comes in. As farmer Alex Liebman puts it, "We want to explore how we can feed ourselves and our community in a saner and less ecologically damaging manner."

With fifteen or so plots scattered around Frogtown and south Minneapolis, this young collective of urban farmers tackles large social and environmental issues head on, from urban development and neighborhood engagement to health and regional connectivity, while also trying to make a fair livelihood.

to me having done this at home and told me that chioggia beets are now in their rotation."

It is only with tight-knit relationships between farmers and chefs like this that late winter conversations about seed varieties, weekly availabilities emails, and text messages about vegetables that are suddenly just right for harvest—"the true expression of the season," as Thomas describes it—can occur and reach customers making decisions about where they spend their money.

CHIOGGIA BEET CARPACCIO WITH WILD MUSHROOM À LA GRECQUE AND GOAT CHEESE FONDUTA

1 medium to large chioggia beet

1 lemon

¹/₂ cup olive oil

1 bunch chives

3 oz. wild mushrooms (chanterelle or maitake are my favorites)

FONDUTA

2 oz. heavy cream

¹/₄ cup goat cheese

1 bunch seasonal garden greens

Sea salt and cracked pepper

Carefully slice uncooked chioggia beet as thin as possible on a mandolin or slicer. Zest and juice the lemon. Make basic vinaigrette by combining lemon juice and olive oil in the ratio of one part juice to three parts oil. Then add half the lemon zest and season with salt, pepper, and chopped chives. Sauté mushrooms and dress with vinaigrette. Coat the beets with vinaigrette and arrange on serving plates. To make the fonduta, add the remaining lemon zest and some cracked pepper to the cream and bring just to a simmer. Whisk in the goat cheese until smooth and cloud-like. You can adjust the consistency with more cream to your liking. Garnish beets with the goat cheese fonduta, sea salt, cracked pepper, mushrooms à la grecque, and garden greens.

EL NORTEÑO

Whole Farm Co-op

Clemen Serna and Estella Guintana, partners in the Mexican restaurant El Norteño, are just doing what comes naturally. "That's how we grew up. We went out to the garden to pick our food, and that's what we ate," says Clemen.

Home for the sisters, before 1990, was Chihuahua, Mexico. "We grew up in a small town; we would grow our own vegetables and eat what was fresh. We know what is good for you," Clemen continues. "And then, ten years ago when we started the restaurant, we met a wonderful man, Tim King. Tim introduced us to many local growers so we could continue with what we know."

Many of the growers Tim introduced the women to are part of the Whole Farm Co-op. The co-op includes more than thirty farm families in central Minnesota who are committed to growing food sustainably. On a regular basis, Whole Farm delivers everything from fresh produce, meats, and cheese to flour and honey to customers in the Twin Cities. Their customers

Clemen Serna and Estella Guintana

include members of churches, colleges and nonprofits, as well as food co-ops and several restaurants. El Norteño is the only restaurant they supply that serves authentic Mexican fare.

Clemen and Estella buy a number of ingredients from Whole Farm Co-op, which they use in their entrees. They lament that it is sometimes hard to get the peppers they need because of Minnesota's short growing season. "It is especially hard to get all your products locally in the winter," says Clemen, "but we do what we can." In the summer, they rejoice in getting fresh cilantro from the garden. "It is so tasty and smells so good," Clemen says.

The food at El Norteño is delicious and the setting friendly and unpretentious, just like Clemen and Estella. It is all made from scratch—the enchiladas, tamales, and chile rellenos, as well as rice and beans. The tortillas, both corn and flour varieties, are always fresh. "If you know what fresh food is, you know the difference, you can taste it," says Clemen. "We know what fresh Mexican food tastes like, and we make it here."

ENCHILADAS SUISAS

Serves 4–6

1 tablespoon vegetable oil
½ lb. tomatillos (husks removed), chopped
1 small onion, chopped
1 garlic clove, minced
4 jalapeño peppers, chopped (the seeds and membrane are
   the hottest part of the pepper; remove it for a milder sauce)
10 corn tortillas
2 cups shredded chicken
1½ cup Chihuahua cheese
1 cup chicken broth
Sour cream, chopped onion, and cilantro, for garnish

To prepare the sauce, simmer tomatillos, garlic, onion, and peppers in vegetable oil for 10 minutes. Process the mixture in a blender (or use an immersion blender) until smooth. Add salt to taste.

Preheat oven to 350°F. Place less than ¼ cup chicken and 2 tablespoons cheese in the center of each tortilla. Roll up and place, center seam down, in a 9x13-inch baking dish. Repeat, using all tortillas and chicken. Pour enchilada sauce over all, sprinkle with additional cheese, and bake for 30 minutes.

Garnish with sour cream, cilantro, and raw onion.

GARDENS OF SALONICA

Hill and Vale Farm, Zweber Farm, Roger's Farm

Sixteen years ago, Anna Christoforides' mother said, "Why are you opening a restaurant *there*? No one will find you!" Many people have found the Gardens of Salonica in northeast Minneapolis, including the restaurant reviewer Zagat, who named the Gardens the second-best Greek restaurant in the nation in 2004. That's a lot of great moussaka.

Anna and Lazaros Christoforides have always been co-op members and use organic, local products personally. But while starting a family and working on their graduate degrees at the University of Minnesota, they couldn't always afford meat. Anna created a vegetarian moussaka—no meat in the budget that week—that inspired Lazoros to exclaim, "People will beat a path to your door for this!" And it's still one of the favorite selections on the current menu.

From student housing to an Uptown Art Fair booth to a shared restaurant kitchen for their growing catering business, in 1991 the Christoforideses, found an unoccupied building in northeast Minneapolis that was available with one year's free rent. With that bonus, and a full year of painting, removing three layers of linoleum, plastering, and creating the artsy decor —no Mediterranean murals on these walls—they opened with seven tables. That was the beginning of the Gardens of Salonica that you see today.

Anna Christoforides

While centuries-old Greek cuisine is the basis of the menu, Anna carefully updates dishes and puts her own twist on things. A customer favorite—boughatsa— is one of these. Greek food lovers will recognize the concept as that found in spanikopita or tyropita—phyllo pastry filled and baked with tasty ingredients. Among the varieties of boughatsa at Gardens of Salonica are leek-skordalia, mushrooms with kefalotyri cheese, and on the sweet side, custard and apricot.

The secret to the food at Gardens of Salonica is the same secret known by all great cooks Greek and non-Greek alike— fresh, wholesome ingredients. There is barely a food-service ingredient used at the restaurant. Hill and Vale Farm in Wykoff and Zweber Farm in Elko provide the meat. All eggs, sugar, and butter are organic, from free-range animals. The herbs and produce come from Roger's Farm. The co-ops provide the honey; the coffee is free-trade Borealis. And the local farmers' market on Larpenteur is a favorite seasonal stop.

Do people realize the effort Anna goes to in order to provide this quality of food? "Probably not," she says, "but just come for the Greek food and you'll realize that something different is happening here."

FASOLAKI ARNI (LAMB AND GREEN BEANS)

Serves 4–6

LAMB

2 lb. all-natural lamb, suitable for braising (bone-in shoulder or ribs)

2 tablespoons olive oil

6 to 10 cloves garlic, sliced

1 cinnamon stick

½ teaspoon salt

½ teaspoon black pepper

1 cup tomato sauce (or fresh tomatoes; see note)

Heat Dutch oven on medium high, add olive oil, and sear all ingredients together except tomato sauce, stirring constantly until browned.

Reduce heat. Add 1 cup tomato sauce (or in summer when tomatoes are ripe, cut 4 tomatoes on the hemisphere, squeeze out and discard seeds, and grate tomatoes over meat until only peel is left. Discard peel.)

Cover and reduce on a very low flame. Stir periodically to ensure that all the meat cooks in contact with the tomatoes. Cook about an hour or until the meat falls off the bone. Remove from heat. Cool.

GREEN BEANS

4 dry white onions, sliced to make 6 cups

2 bay leaves

1 teaspoon dry organic basil

1 teaspoon salt

1 teaspoon black pepper

2 lb. fresh green beans with trimmed ends; or frozen green beans, at room temperature

2 cups fresh diced skinless tomatoes

In a separate Dutch oven, heat ½ cup pure olive oil. Cook onions with all the spices until they are translucent.

Add the green beans and stir, cooking the beans until they just start to turn from bright green to army green. Then add the tomatoes. Cover and reduce heat until desired texture of the beans is reached. Greek cooks tend to cook beans until they are very soft.

ASSEMBLY

Lift lamb and tomatoes out of the Dutch oven with a slotted spoon and add to green beans. Simmer an additional 10 minutes until flavors blend. Adjust salt and pepper to taste.

Serve with crusty peasant bread and chunks of feta.

TOURLOU

Delicious hot or at room temperature.

Serves 4–5

½ cup extra virgin olive oil

2 medium onions, sliced

1 small fennel bulb with fronds, sliced (discard leaves)

¼ cup sliced garlic

½ teaspoon salt

½ teaspoon black pepper

¼ cup fresh basil, chopped (or 1 teaspoon dry basil)

2 bay leaves

4 cups eggplant, cubed

4 cups zucchini, cut into 1-inch rounds

4 cups green beans (with ends trimmed)

2 cups tomatoes (fresh chopped or canned sauce)

Preheat oil in large sauté pan or Dutch oven. Add onions, fennel bulb, and seasonings. Sauté until onions wilt. Add garlic. Continue sautéing until onions and garlic are soft and transparent. Add eggplant, stirring to coat with oil and seasonings. Cook about 5 minutes, stirring periodically. Add zucchini and green beans. Stir to coat. Reduce flame/heat to medium low and cover.

Cook until green beans start to change color (bright green to army green). Add tomatoes; stir in gently. Cover and simmer until cooked to preference.

Serve with feta and crusty peasant bread.

RIZOGALO (RICE PUDDING)

Serves 4

1 quart organic 2% (or whole) milk

½ cup uncooked jasmine rice

1 cinnamon stick

1 teaspoon organic lemon zest

Heat to simmer over medium high, stirring frequently. Simmer and stir until slightly thickened and rice rises to surface and stays (about 30 minutes). Add scant ½ cup organic sugar. Heat additional 5 minutes. Cool and serve.

HEARTLAND RESTAURANT AND FARM DIRECT MARKET

Cedar Summit

Heartland owner Lenny Russo won't try to "force feed" his way of doing things on anyone, but when he does express himself—which he'll do quite freely—it's fun to partake in the feast of how and why he cooks the way he does.

Heartland, which Lenny co-owns with his wife, Mega Hoehn, originated from a desire to feature North American Midwest cuisine, using ingredients made by artisan producers or raised by small family farmers who use either organic or natural farming methods. In 2010, they expanded into a much larger space in Lowertown. This change also included the addition of their Farm Direct Market, where diners and neighbors alike can take home the same high-quality fresh and value-added products used in the restaurant, from Cedar Summit milk to house-made charcuterie. Lenny explains, "When you're a chef, you're relating to people in the most fundamental way, giving them sustenance. You bear a certain responsibility to give them healthful food. I take that responsibility seriously, and the connection to how the food is produced goes right along with that responsibility."

Lenny's standards are high. "If a farmer shows up with a bag of beans at my door, I'm not necessarily going to buy them, I want to know how they're grown," he says. "You have to be a farmer with some integrity to work with me. I'm always asking the questions . . . are you rotating your crops? Are your animals being grazed, and how are they treated?"

Lenny likes buying from Hill and Vale Farm because he knows that owners Joe and Bonnie Austin are careful to nurture biodiversity on their rolling pastures near Wykoff. He likes Thousand Hills Cattle Company, not only because of their high-quality beef, but also because the small company is playing an important role in bringing like-minded farmers together to meet a growing demand for pasture-raised beef.

Working as partners with his farmers and producers is vital to a sustainable relationship. Sometimes a small farmer will need more for his product than a larger farm would need. Some chefs can't afford to do that. If a chef is working for someone else, part of the job is to maximize profits. Lenny wants to pay the price that allows for the farmer to get his product to the restaurant, make a living, and support the farm.

"Of course, when you're chef/owner, your measure of success is different than someone that wants to make a lot of money," Lenny says. "My measure of success is that all the bills are paid and there's money in the bank. In my case, this is what I do and how I fulfill myself. I don't need to get rich, because I'm rich just being here."

Lenny has a national reputation as a purist—as owning a restaurant that represents the best of the Midwest might indicate. He says, "I don't know why people come here. They may be interested in my issues, they may like the food, or they may just live around the corner and it's a convenient place to eat, but hopefully, they leave with the message and are satisfied.

MIDWESTERN CASSOULET

Lenny suggests using Kramarczuk's Polish ham sausage, called Krakovska, or any good garlic pork sausage. Kramarczuk is located in northeast Minneapolis.

COOKED WHITE BEANS

1 lb. great northern white beans, rinsed and checked for stones

1 smoked pork hock (½ lb. smoked bacon, diced into ¼-inch chunks, may be substituted)

1 sweet onion, peeled and studded with cloves

1 large carrot, peeled

1 bouquet garni consisting of 2 parsley sprigs, 2 thyme sprigs, 1 bay leaf, 2 garlic cloves, and 15 black peppercorns

Soak the beans overnight, making sure there is twice the water as there are beans by volume. Drain and place in a pot with the other ingredients. Pour in enough cold water so it is again twice the volume of the beans. Bring the pot to a boil over high heat. Reduce the heat to a simmer, and gently cook the beans until they are tender but not splitting (about 1½ hours).

Drain the beans, making sure to reserve the cooking liquid for further use. Remove the vegetables and the bouquet garni. Turn the beans out onto a sheet pan and allow to cool. Separate the meat from the pork hock; discard the bone. Return the meat to the beans.

RAGOÛT

2 lbs. sweet onions, peeled and diced into ¼-inch pieces

10 garlic cloves

½ cup rendered duck fat (or rendered pork fat or whole unsalted butter)

4 lb. lean pork, diced into ¼-inch chunks

2 lb. white wine garlic sausage, cooked and bias sliced

2 lb. Cooked White Beans (recipe above)

½ gallon brown chicken or meat stock (or equal amount of reserved bean cooking liquid)

2 cups reserved bean cooking liquid

4 Roma tomatoes or 2 large tomatoes (must be ripe), peeled, seeded, and chopped

2 tablespoons tomato paste

1 each bouquet garni consisting of 2 parsley sprigs, 2 thyme sprigs, 1 bay leaf, and 1 whole nutmeg

1 tablespoon sea salt

1 teaspoon Tellicherry black pepper, freshly ground

Brown the onions and garlic in the duck fat in a shallow, non-reactive saucepot or brazier (5-quart shallow saucepan, 6x14-inch) over medium-high heat. Add the pork and sausage. Cook for ten minutes until the pork is well browned; add the beans. Pour in the stock and the reserved cooking liquid. When the ragoût begins to simmer, stir in the tomatoes and the tomato paste. Add the bouquet garni and season the ragoût with the salt and pepper. Cover the pan and continue to simmer for one hour. The ragout may be cooled and served at a later time at this point. This will allow time for the flavors to blend.

To serve, spoon some of the ragoût into an oven-safe baking crock. Top generously with fresh bread crumbs and dot the top with some small knobs of rendered fat or whole unsalted butter. Bake in a 400°F oven until the cassoulet begins to bubble. Remove and serve immediately.

FRESH VEGETABLE SLAW

Serves 6–8

⅓ lb. Savoy cabbage, cored and thinly sliced

⅓ lb. red cabbage, cored and thinly sliced

⅓ lb. fresh fennel bulb, cored and thinly sliced

⅓ lb. turnips, finely julienned

⅓ lb. table carrots, peeled and finely julienned

⅓ lb. sweet onions, thinly sliced

1 cup grapeseed oil

⅓ cup apple cider vinegar

¾ tablespoons fine sea salt

1½ teaspoons Tellicherry black pepper, freshly ground

3 tablespoons fresh flat-leaf parsley, chopped

3 tablespoons fresh tarragon leaves, chopped

Combine all of the ingredients in a non-reactive mixing bowl. Toss well, making sure all of the ingredients are well blended.

ASPARAGUS-BARLEY RISOTTO

This dish may be served as an accompaniment for chicken or fish or may be served as a vegetarian entrée.

Serves 6–8

1 quart Court-Bouillon (recipe below); you may also use organic vegetable or chicken stock
2 tablespoons grapeseed oil
1 white onion, peeled and diced into ⅛-inch pieces
1 carrot, peeled and diced into ⅛-inch pieces
2 ribs celery, peeled and diced into ⅛-inch pieces
1 clove garlic, minced
½ lb. hulled barley
2 cups asparagus, bias cut and blanched
1 tablespoon fresh thyme leaves
2 tablespoons unsalted butter
¼ cup fresh Parmesan cheese, grated
1 teaspoon fine sea salt, or to taste
½ teaspoon black pepper, freshly ground, or to taste

Bring the bouillon to a slow simmer in a non-reactive pot. Meanwhile, heat the grapeseed oil in a shallow braising pan or saucepan over medium-low heat. Add the vegetables and garlic and lightly sauté until tender. Add the barley and season it with the salt and pepper. Sauté the barley with the vegetables until it begins to change color, stirring occasionally with a wooden spoon. This is called pearlizing.

Once the barley is pearlized, slowly add the bouillon using a 4-ounce ladle. Continue to stir the barley as you add the stock. Allow the stock to become completely absorbed before adding another ladleful. Repeat this process until all of the stock is used. The barley should be tender but not soft.

Add the asparagus and thyme and remove the risotto from the heat. Continue to stir gently until the asparagus is warmed through. Gently stir in the butter and the cheese and adjust the salt and pepper if necessary.

COURT-BOUILLON
Yield: 1 gallon. Preparation time: 2½ hours

2 white onions, peeled and diced into ¼-inch pieces
3 carrots, peeled and diced into ¼-inch pieces
½ stalk celery, peeled and diced into ¼-inch pieces
1 medium leek, cleaned and diced into ¼-inch pieces
1 garlic bulb, quartered
2 tablespoons grapeseed oil
1 cup dry white wine
1 bouquet garni consisting of 2 thyme sprigs, 2 marjoram sprigs, 3 parsley sprigs, 1 bay leaf, 5 whole allspice, 10 white peppercorns, 10 black peppercorns, and 12 fennel seeds

In a stock pot over moderate heat, sweat the vegetables and garlic in the grapeseed oil until tender. Add the white wine and the bouquet garni. Fill the pot with one gallon of cold water and bring it to a boil over a high flame. Reduce the heat and simmer for two hours, skimming intermittently. Strain through a fine mesh strainer lined with moistened cheesecloth.

Florence and Dave Minar

GREEN GAZPACHO WITH DILL SOUR CREAM

Know your peppers! Early season jalapeños may be too mild, and late-season peppers may be too spicy. This is a well-balanced sweet-and-spicy dish—don't overdo it.

GAZPACHO

1 cup honeydew melon, peeled and seeded

1 tablespoon jalapeño peppers, gilled and seeded

¼ cup green bell peppers, gilled and seeded

¼ cup green onions, chopped

½ cup cucumbers, seeded and chopped

1 cup tomatillos, husked and chopped

1 cup sweet onions, peeled and diced into ¼-inch pieces

2 tablespoons Banyuls vinegar or other red wine vinegar

2 tablespoons fresh Italian parsley, chopped

1 tablespoon fine sea salt

½ teaspoon white pepper, freshly ground

Purée the fruits and vegetables with the remaining ingredients in a high-speed blender until smooth. Transfer to a labeled container with a tight-fitting lid and refrigerate immediately.

DILL SOUR CREAM

1 cup sour cream

2 tablespoons fresh dill, chopped

½ teaspoon sea salt, or more, to season to taste

½ teaspoon Tellicherry black pepper, freshly ground

Mix all of the ingredients thoroughly in a stainless steel mixing bowl until well blended.

To plate, ladle six ounces of gazpacho into a chilled serving bowl. Garnish with sour cream and some freshly chopped chives.

HELL'S KITCHEN

Silver Bison Ranch

Mitch Omer, and his business partner, Steve Meyer, will tell you that they named their restaurant Hell's Kitchen because that is what it feels like amid the simmering pots, hot ovens, and bustle that comes with making food from scratch for a hungry crowd of customers. While Mitch and Steve have been known to be irreverent at times, they are pious when it comes to food.

Mitch Omer and Steve Meyer

Hell's Kitchen serves up creative and hearty breakfasts and lunches, which include things like ricotta-lemon pancakes and a walleye BLT. Mitch and Steve take good ingredients seriously and believe that homemade is always best. That is why not only is the food made from scratch, but so is the ketchup, mustard, marmalade, iced tea, tomato juice, and hot cocoa. Their homemade peanut butter won such rave reviews on National Public Radio's *Splendid Table* that they even had to start selling it online to keep up with demand.

It is not surprising that Mitch insists on the best-quality ingredients for the restaurant. Over the years, Mitch has developed relationships with a few local purveyors that, Mitch says, "I will

never leave." One of these is the Silver Bison Ranch in Baldwin, Wisconsin.

"I have been buying naturally fed and individually culled bison from Loren and Marilyn Smeester since long before I opened Hell's Kitchen," Mitch notes. After being reviewed in several magazines and newspapers about serving bison meat, Mitch says that every other bison rancher in a 500-mile radius wanted to sell to him. He explains, "But I have a personal relationship with this purveyor, this rancher, this friend. I will never buy bison from anyone else but them, and I will always have bison on my menus."

Another favorite ingredient that Hell's Kitchen buys direct is hand-harvested, wood-parched wild rice. They buy this exclusively from the Leech Lake Band of Ojibwe. "There is no other product, anywhere, that compares with this," he says. He uses the wild rice for his Mahnomin Porridge, which is an adaptation of a journal entry he first read about years ago while studying the writings of fur trappers from the 1800s. He explains, "It was recorded that French trappers observed northern Indians eating a meal of cooked wild rice with nuts, berries, and maple syrup." Mitch played around with those ingredients and finally perfected his recipe by adding heavy cream.

"When we first opened, no one would order the porridge," says Mitch. "It just seemed so foreign." But he was determined not to drop the item from the menu and began giving away samples for customers to try. His strategy worked. Mitch says, "I used to buy fifty pounds of wild rice every two or three months. Now I buy nearly fifty pounds a week to keep up with demand." The recipe for the Mahnomen porridge is one that is most requested by customers.

Using local foods is not a religion at Hell's Kitchen, but when they find the right local purveyor — it's a match made in heaven. As Mitch says about his bison and wild rice suppliers, "I'm practically married to these guys!"

MAPLE-GLAZED BISON SAUSAGE

This slightly spicy, maple syrup–sweetened sausage is the perfect accompaniment to a Hell's Kitchen breakfast, and a key ingredient in the restaurant's sausage bread. As the raw patty is charcoal-grilled, the maple syrup caramelizes on the outside, sealing in the natural juices and preserving the flavor of this wonderful meat.

Makes approximately eight 3-oz. patties

1 lb. ground bison
$\frac{1}{4}$ cup minced shallots
$\frac{1}{4}$ cup pure maple syrup
2 tablespoons minced garlic
2 teaspoons ground sage
2 teaspoons red pepper flakes
2 teaspoons fennel seed
1 teaspoon dried thyme
1 teaspoon ground white pepper
1 teaspoon kosher salt

Place all ingredients in a mixer fitted with a paddle and slowly blend together until just mixed. Do not over-mix the ingredients because this will compact the sausage and make for a tougher, drier product. With moist hands, patty the sausage mixture into 3-oz. portions.

Bison meat is so low in fat that these patties should be cooked no longer than 4 minutes per side. If charcoal broiling, you should cook the patties over a medium-high heat on a rack set 4 inches from the hot coals. For stovetop cooking, use a heavy skillet lightly oiled, and preferably cast iron. These sausage patties should cook over high heat.

Cook the sausages about 4 minutes per side. As mentioned earlier, Hell's Kitchen chefs cook their sausages over a charcoal grill. However, sautéing them in a skillet produces a juicier sausage because the patties cook in their own juices, instead of those juices dripping away through a grill grate. And never press down with a spatula on the sausages while they cook, since this pushes the flavorful juices out of the patties.

MAHNOMIN PORRIDGE

When Mitch Omer and Steve Meyer first opened Hell's Kitchen in 2002, they couldn't give this away. Yet Mitch so loved this porridge, he refused to give up on it and decided to give away tiny samples of it in espresso cups. Now word has spread like wildfire, and this porridge is one of Hell's Kitchen's top sellers.

Serves 4

4 cups cooked wild rice
$\frac{1}{2}$ cup roasted, cracked hazelnuts
$\frac{1}{4}$ cup sweetened dried cranberries
$\frac{1}{4}$ cup dried blueberries
$\frac{1}{4}$ cup pure maple syrup
1 cup heavy whipping cream

In a heavy, non-stick saucepan, add the cooked wild rice, hazelnuts, blueberries, cranberries, and maple syrup and cook over medium-high heat, about 3 minutes. Add the heavy cream and, stirring constantly, heat through, about 2 minutes. Ladle into bowls and serve immediately.

BISON SAUSAGE BREAD

This is a batter bread, rich and dense, and utilizing one of Mitch Omer's favorite foods in the world, bison. People might find it an odd recipe, using ground meat and coffee, but Mitch guarantees, once people try this, they will be hooked forever. This is best eaten browned in a toaster or grilled, and slathered in sweet cream butter. This is a meal unto itself.

Makes 1 loaf

10 oz. maple-glazed bison sausage; Italian sausage can be substituted
¾ cup dried blueberries
¾ cup dark roast prepared coffee
4 large eggs
¾ cup walnut pieces, toasted
¾ cup granulated sugar
½ lb. dark brown sugar
2 cups all-purpose flour
1 teaspoon baking powder
1 teaspoon baking soda
1 teaspoon cinnamon
1 teaspoon ground ginger
¼ teaspoon nutmeg
⅛ teaspoon ground cloves

Preheat oven to 350°F. In the bowl of an electric mixer fitted with a paddle, add the sausage, dried blueberries, and coffee and mix together slowly until well blended. Slowly add the eggs, one at a time, while slowly mixing.

Stop the mixer and add the remaining ingredients. Slowly beat together for 3 to 4 minutes, or until well blended. Stop the mixer and with a rubber spatula, scrape the bottom and sides of the mixing bowl. Beat another 2 to 3 minutes on medium speed.

Butter and flour a 5x9-inch loaf pan. Scrape the batter into the pan and bake about 1½ hours on the center rack of the oven. Test for doneness. Allow the bread to rest for 10 minutes in the pan; remove to a cooling rack. When cooled to room temperature, wrap the bread and refrigerate or freeze.

To serve, cut into thick slices, butter, and grill on a flat pan; or toast and serve well-buttered.

LUCIA'S RESTAURANT, LUCIA'S WINE BAR, AND LUCIA'S TO GO

Fischer Farm

While Lucia Watson is often referred to as the pioneer of the local food movement in Minnesota, she tends to think of herself more as going "back to the future." Lucia and her customers are moving out of the glitch we've been in since the post–World War II boom, when many people quit eating locally and healthfully. It's been a three-generation glitch!

A third-generation Minnesotan, Lucia's grandmother, Lucia Louise—"Lulu"—instilled the value of food in her. These days, Lucia is reminded of these traditions when she visits the farmers' markets in France. "When the market is in full swing, they still sell live rabbits, chickens, and pigeons, but only the older women are buying them," Lucia says. "When that generation goes, I don't think they'll be selling that way. That will be a sad day for a country that has always placed such value on their food and traditions."

While Lucia doesn't buy her chicken with the feathers on, she does buy the freshest ingredients she can find. Pork comes from Fischer Farms in Waseca. Vegetables come from Riverbend and other local farms.

Lucia has received many awards for her efforts to promote good local food. She is a board member of Youth Farm and

Lucia Watson

Market and an advocate of programs that teach youth about growing and cooking food. "When you see how differently kids approach food when they know more about it, it's just amazing," she says. "I taught a class where we were going to make peanut butter. The kids did not believe that it came from peanuts. That's such a symbol of how we've become disconnected between our food and where it comes from."

So what does Lucia suggest we do about it? "Consumers should expand their definition of local," she says. "If you randomly interviewed people, their ideas of local food are tomatoes, lettuce, and corn. The truth is, if you committed to buying all-local milk for one year, you would be making more of a difference in the local economy than going to the farmers' market every Saturday for the whole summer.

"Look at what's available locally. There's a lot in Minnesota—flour, butter, and wonderful cheese. Commit to getting a freezer; put twenty chickens, a quarter of a cow, a lamb in it. And then you have a really good local thing going, like my grandma Lulu. I just encourage people to take that first step."

BEER BATTER WALLEYE FINGERS WITH
MAPLE-MUSTARD DIPPING SAUCE

The batter here is just a little bit different, an alternative to thinner mixes. Meanwhile, the simple maple-mustard dipping sauce is one of my all-time favorites. I use walleye to do this recipe, but any lean fish works just as well. Perhaps my overall favorite is perch.

Serves 1–2

½ cup flour
Salt and pepper to taste
¼ teaspoon baking powder
¼ teaspoon dry mustard
½ teaspoon cayenne powder
½ cup beer (room temperature)
Oil for frying
2 walleye fillets, bones removed, cut into fingers or appropriate
   portions

Combine the flour, salt, pepper, baking powder, mustard, and cayenne in a bowl. Add the beer and whisk. If you use cold beer, let the batter sit for an hour after mixing.

In a heavy pot, heat the oil to 350°F. Test the oil by sprinkling a few drops of batter into it. The batter droplets should sizzle and immediately rise to the top of the oil.

Dip the fish in the batter and thoroughly coat each fillet. Fry until crisp and golden, about 3 to 5 minutes. Remove with a slotted spoon and drain on paper towels.

MAPLE-MUSTARD DIPPING SAUCE

½ cup smooth Dijon mustard
3 tablespoons maple syrup

Mix together and taste for seasoning.

PORKETTA (GARLIC-FENNEL PORK ROAST)

Porketta is of Italian origin, but this garlic-studded, fennel-flavored, long-cooked roast has been adapted by everyone—Finn, Norwegian, and Cornish alike—who grew up on the Iron Range, the iron-mining area of northern Minnesota. Its very mention will elicit tender declarations from even the most stoic north woodsman.

This recipe was inspired by Margaret Erjavec of Virginia, Minnesota, who contributed it to *The Old Country Cookbook*. You may want to adjust the seasonings according to your own tastes. The meat must be cooked until it falls apart when touched with a fork. Porketta should not be sliced, but pulled apart. It is wonderful served with roasted potatoes at supper and is even better the next day or the day after, when eaten between slices of homemade bread.

Serves 8–10

1 boneless pork butt roast (6 lb.)
2 teaspoons salt
2 tablespoons freshly ground black pepper
10 cloves garlic, coarsely chopped
1 cup chopped fresh parsley
½ cup fennel seeds
¼ cup olive oil
1 large fennel bulb, finely chopped
6 new potatoes, cut into large chunks
2 stalks celery, cut into chunks
6 carrots, cut into chunks
2 medium onions, peeled and cut into chunks

Cut the roast in half lengthwise and open it like a book. Combine all of the seasoning ingredients with the olive oil and rub it over both sides of the meat, pressing the fennel seeds and garlic into the meat. Spread the chopped fennel bulb over the meat, then fold the meat back together or roll it up and secure with a string. Place the meat in a roasting pan, cover, and bake in a preheated 325°F oven for 3 to 4 hours. Toward the last 30 minutes of cooking, scatter the vegetables on the bottom of the roasting pan and continue cooking the roast until it falls apart when touched with a fork.

Remove the roast from the pan and allow it to sit about 5 minutes before pulling it apart to serve with the vegetables.

ALEXIS BAILLY VINEYARD

Northern Lights Cheese

Alexis Bailly is Minnesota's oldest winery, having opened in the late 1970s. It was the dream of David A. Bailly who, amidst skeptics, set out to develop a great Minnesota wine. On his death in 1990, David's daughter Nan took over the winery and has continued his legacy of making award-winning wines. From bold red wines, such as Voyageur, to sweet ice wines, such as Isis, Alexis Bailly has been a pioneer in Minnesota's growing wine industry.

"My father was the original pioneer" explains Nan Bailly. Her father, David A. Bailly, defied skeptics when he planted Minnesota's first vineyard in Hastings. "His inspiration came twofold," she describes. "One, he had a lot of ambition and passion with the wine, working with his hands getting into the soil and two, he was inspired by the progressive movement of hybridization."

In fact, Nan's father's efforts predated modern experiments and research at the University of Minnesota, which have since yielded more hardy vines for Minnesota's climate. "When he planted his vineyard in 1973 there wasn't really anyone doing viticulture outside of the norm . . . I remember a headline in a Minneapolis publication once called us Freak Vitners." Yet his commitment and trailblazing spirit led to success in what is considered one of the most challenging climates. In 1977, the vineyard celebrated the release of its first commercial vintage. The following year's Léon Millot release won a gold medal from New York's Wineries Unlimited; successive vintages continued to win numerous awards.

In 1978, Alexis Bailly opened their tasting room, which now attracts visitors from all over Minnesota and Wisconsin. "I always say we're closer than France and cheaper than Napa," jokes Nan. Despite her father's focus on the pure craft of winemaking, the tourism aspect has become vital to the vineyard, establishing a new genre for wineries whose agricultural success is challenged by severe winters. "We provide people with that niche, where you can come and you can experience the beauty, the romantic idea of a vineyard, the experience of a winery—the whole atmosphere. People think about the lifestyle in Europe and fantasize about it . . . you know, *A Day in Tuscany* or *A Year in Provence*. If you just look over our shoulder we have that exact same thing here. You just need to be aware of your surroundings."

When Nan succeeded her father as winemaker for Alexis Bailly Vineyards, she worked in the vineyards and focused on not just the craft but also on building relationships with her

Nan Bailly

customers and partners. "What I've learned over the years is what my customers want to do here, they want to do what I like to do on my farm." Nan encourages her visitors to relax and spend the day. "I think it's healthier and safer to have a picnic, eat something, do something recreational, or not! Sit under a tree and read a book. It's all about just being able to enjoy the atmosphere that the winery and the vineyard create." She encourages her guests to linger and take advantage of the vineyard's many offerings. After visiting the tasting room, her guests can explore the vineyards, a restored natural prairie, sculpture park, bocce ball courts, and beautiful picnic areas.

Nan sells an assortment of food to accompany her wine, including a wide variety of locally made cheeses, including Northern Lights Blue. Cheesemaker Joe Sherman can trace his legacy back to the very first blue cheese producer in the United States, Felix Frederickson, who founded Treasure Cave in 1936. "In the early 1980s I gained employment at the facility in Faribault," Joe says. "There was a gentleman there that was a 20 to 30 year cheese maker; his name was Ray Eljer. Ray taught me how to make blue, and Ray was taught by Felix. That stretches me way back a long time ago."

Northern Lights Blue was born out of Joe's experience in Faribault, which he has expanded on with specialty ingredients and a small, hands-on process. "I use the best milk available to me, which is Brown Swiss milk from Arthurst Farm in Plato, Minnesota. It is a small boutique farm that has about seventy head, and this wonderful Brown Swiss milk." Bred for cheesemaking, Brown Swiss cows yield milk with a higher fat and protein content than the ubiquitous Holstein. Joe adds further distinction to his cheese by using a fine Italian sea salt and extending his aging process to twice that of most blue cheeses. As a result, Northern Lights Blue has "a piquant taste against sweet creamy background. It is a widely appealing cheese, peppery and without the overbearing pungency of some of the blues."

"Joe has blue in his veins," jokes Nan. She frequently invites him to the vineyard to present his cheese at her biannual wine pairing event, which matches the best of regional, handmade food with Alexis Bailly wines. Of course the wine tends to steal the show. The premium wine is called Voyageur; the name harkens back to the pioneering French Canadians who faced challenging conditions paddling the region in their birchbarked canoes. Nan views this also as metaphor for Minnesota wine-making and an honor to her pioneering father.

"Joe's cheese," says Nan, "just goes perfect with that wine."

ALEXIS BAILLY VINEYARD'S SANGRIA

Serves 6

Served at "Jazz in the Vineyard" events every Sunday afternoon in July and August.

1 bottle ABV Rose Noir (for a lighter version)
   or ABV Country Red (for a drier version)
$^1/_2$ cup ABV Ratafia Dessert Wine
$^1/_4$ cup sugar

1 orange, sliced in half-moon slices
$^1/_2$ lemon, sliced in half-moon slices
Club soda or lemon-lime soda (optional)
Frozen grapes or blueberries (optional)

Combine everything in a pitcher, dissolving sugar in the wine by stirring gently. Mash the orange and lemon slices lightly with the back of a spoon. Add to the wine and soak fruit in the wine for at least one hour, or up to overnight in the refrigerator. Serve chilled over ice, or substitute frozen grapes or blueberries. Top with soda, if desired.

MULLED WINE

Yields 5 5-oz servings

A delicious way to warm up your winter!

1 bottle ABV Rose Noir
$^1/_4$ to $^1/_2$ cup sugar (adjust to your taste)
Peel of $^1/_2$ an orange
$^1/_2$ of a cinnamon stick
4 green cardamon pods, lightly crushed (optional)
$^1/_2$ teaspoons whole cloves
1 teaspoons vanilla extract

Heat wine to a low simmer, dissolving sugar. Add all ingredients and continue to simmer for at least 30 minutes, being careful not to boil. Strain before serving. Alternately, place spices in cheesecloth for easy removal before serving.

NAN'S ROASTED ALMONDS

Yields 1 cup

This is a wine-friendly recipe for both red and whites. Add spiced olives and a piece of cheese, such as Northern Lights Blue, and you have a lovely, easy way to relax and enjoy the end of a day.

1 tablespoon unsalted Hope butter
1 cup raw almonds
1 teaspoon minced fresh rosemary
1 teaspoon Kosher salt

Heat oven to 350°F. Melt the butter in a saucepan over medium-low heat on the stovetop. Add the almonds, rosemary, and salt and toss to coat. Spread the almonds evenly on a cookie sheet and bake for 8 to 10 minutes until toasted, careful not to burn.

SPICED OLIVES

Yields 3 cups

2 tablespoons olive oil
2 cloves garlic, chopped fine
$^1/_2$ tablespoon whole coriander seeds
2 teaspoons fennel seeds
3 cups kalamata olives (or a mix of fine, cured olives)

Sauté the garlic and olive oil together for 1 minute on medium heat, careful not to brown the garlic. Add the coriander and fennel seeds and toast for one more minute, stirring constantly. Add the olives and heat until warm. Serve as an appetizer with Alexis Bailly Vineyard Seyval Blanc white table wine.

Northern Lights Blue Cheese

MINNESOTA LANDSCAPE ARBORETUM AND GOOD LIFE CATERING

The minute you start talking to Jenny Breen you know that she is an educator. Not a preacher, an educator. She bubbles over with information that is passed on in her cooking classes at the Minnesota Landscape Arboretum and through her style of catering in her company, Good Life Catering.

"I love teaching people to cook. It gives me an opportunity to connect, to share the love and joy of cooking, and the pleasure of eating good food and being a responsible consumer. . . . I love to show that to people," says Jenny.

The Arboretum is a perfect fit for Jenny's philosophy of food. In recent years, the Arboretum has worked to educate people about where food comes from and now is focusing on local food products and the people behind them.

"Food that is grown by local farmers just tastes better," is Jenny's mantra. "And, even if your taste buds aren't telling you that, why not put your money behind sustainably grown food?" she adds. "Some of our palates may need to be retrained. We're not accustomed to the leaner taste of grass-fed beef, but no one can tell me that a freshly picked Minnesota-grown carrot isn't candy sweet."

Jenny Breen

That joy of biting into a freshly picked vegetable is something that Jenny loves to share with children. At the Arboretum's kids cooking classes, young cooks pick items from a garden outside the door of the cooking classroom and then prepare their meal. "You'll rarely find a kid that doesn't like green beans that they've picked or grown themselves," Jenny says. All food comes from plants, one way or another. The Arboretum and Jenny teach that.

Jenny and the Arboretum are launching a new venture with Green Routes to bring people even closer to their food. Together they will offer culinary tours where participants will visit farms, wineries, and artisan food-makers and then use the bounty they collect to make a meal together, with Jenny's help.

While not a big-time gardener herself, Jenny is a firm believer in preserving the summer and fall bounty for use the rest of the year. Her freezer is full of soups, tomatoes, pesto, and other vegetables. "Freeze or can your food, the way people have done for years," she recommends. "Think ahead and be intentional in your eating. Intentionality around eating is the basis for it all. You have to get back to connecting with your food," she adds.

GRILLED GOUDA SANDWICH WITH ROASTED BEETS AND ARUGULA

Serves 6 as a meal, 12 as an appetizer

1 loaf hearty whole grain bread, sliced thin (enough for 6 full sandwiches, 12 appetizer portions if cut in half)

¼ lb. unsalted butter

1 lb. Eichten, Pastureland, or Gouda cheese of your choice, sliced thin; smoked Gouda works well also

4 medium beets, peeled and sliced thin lengthwise

¼ cup olive oil

¼ cup balsamic vinegar

1 teaspoon salt

½ lb. arugula

Stone-ground mustard

Heat oven to 400°F. Cover beets in olive oil, balsamic vinegar, and salt, and roast in oven, stirring occasionally. Meanwhile, brush outsides of bread with butter, and insides with mustard. When beets are nicely tender, about 30 minutes, remove from oven. Remove from pan and reserve remaining liquid. Assemble sandwiches with a layer of arugula, a layer of beets, and a few slices of cheese over the top. To melt cheese, place open-faced sandwiches on baking pan and place in oven or in covered pan on medium heat. Remove when cheese is melted (about 1 minute). Drizzle with reserved oil and vinegar mixture from beets.

THREE SISTERS SALAD

Serves 6

2 cups pearled barley, cooked in 4 cups water

½ cup water

2 cups corn kernels (frozen or fresh off the cob)

1 lb. green beans, trimmed and cut into 2-inch pieces

1 small red onion, sliced thin

1 red bell pepper, sliced

1 cup dried tomatoes, sliced and re-hydrated in hot water

1 lb. cleaned, trimmed mustard leaves, baby spinach leaves, or other greens

Cook barley until tender; set aside. Heat water and steam corn and green beans until bright, about 2 minutes. Cool immediately under cold water. Combine barley with all vegetables and greens.

DRESSING

½ cup olive oil

¼ cup cider vinegar

¼ cup raspberry vinegar

2 tablespoons stone-ground mustard

2 tablespoons honey

¼ cup fresh dill, chopped

4 cloves garlic, minced

2 teaspoons salt

Prepare dressing by combining all ingredients and whisking well. Pour half of dressing over salad mixture and add more according to taste.

SPOONRIVER RESTAURANT

Mill City Farmers' Market

While in her teens, Brenda Langton worked at a co-op vegetarian restaurant in St. Paul. At the age of twenty, she ventured off to Europe for a year, where markets, restaurants, and cooking with the local ingredients are a way of life. When she returned, she opened Cafe Kardamena in St. Paul, a gourmet vegetarian and seafood restaurant.

A few years later, Brenda visited the Greens Restaurant in San Francisco. "Greens served beautiful vegetarian food that was grown on their own farm," she reminisces. Brenda was inspired and left with the idea of starting a restaurant in Minnesota that also sourced ingredients from local farmers; thus the eponymous Café Brenda was born.

"We've been a part of the community for over 35 years," says Brenda. "My commitment to eating healthy, natural food is just about feeling good and keeping our bodies and minds healthy. I think the best way to teach people is by letting them eat whole grains, beans, seasonal vegetables, farm-fresh chicken and responsibly harvested seafood. We now offer grass-fed beef, so we're not strictly vegetarian and haven't been for years, but people still tend to think of us that way."

Brenda's expansion to Spoonriver, near the new Guthrie Theater, created yet another unexpected venture—the Mill City Farmers' Market. She had planned to start a small farmers' market on the plaza next to Spoonriver when the building manager suggested she take a look at the train shed instead. Brenda realized it would be the perfect place. Mill City Farmers' Market became an overnight success, with over forty-five local vendors providing fresh and flavorful food. In 2009, after twenty-three years, Brenda closed Café Brenda to focus on Spoonriver and the farmers' market.

"With the market, I think people understand more of who I am and what I believe in," says Brenda. "We get people in from all over. They want to understand and to learn more about things like CSAs (community supported agriculture). Did you know we have more CSAs in Minnesota than any other state? How cool is that?"

With a CSA, a person or family buys a "share" from a local farm. Then they get a box of freshly harvested, locally grown food (usually vegetables, but sometimes eggs, flowers, honey, etc.) each week during the growing season. The variety of produce changes with the season, and customers share the risk with the farmer.

"CSAs are a great way to learn to cook with what you have," Brenda explains. "One week you'll get strawberries and asparagus; later in the year, tomatoes and squash. It forces you to think outside of the grocery-store-box mindset. Cook as simply as you can. Braise your greens with a little olive oil and goat cheese. Embrace Asian and Mediterranean styles of cooking, or simple Italian noodles. . . . That's comfort food. It's easy on digestion and delicious. Everything in moderation, even meat!"

With a CSA, a person or family buys a "share" from a local farm. Then they get a box of freshly harvested, locally grown food (usually vegetables, but sometimes eggs, flowers, honey, and so on) each week during the growing season. The variety of produce changes with the season, and customers share the risk with the farmer.

"CSAs are a great way to learn to cook with what you have," Brenda explains. "One week you'll get strawberries and asparagus; later in the year, tomatoes and squash. It forces you to think outside of the grocery-store-box mindset. Cook as simply as you can. Braise your greens with a little olive oil and goat cheese. Embrace Asian and Mediterranean styles of cooking, or simple Italian noodles. . . . That's comfort food. It's easy on digestion and delicious. Everything in moderation, even meat!"

EAST INDIAN POTATO AND PEA PASTRIES

Makes 10

FILLING

4 potatoes, medium cut into 1- to 2-inch chunks; this
   should equal 4 to 5 cups

1 tablespoon olive oil

2 teaspoons coriander seeds

3/4 cup onion, diced

2 jalepeño or serano chilies, minced

1 1/2 teaspoons grated fresh ginger (or 1 teaspoon dried)

1 cup frozen peas, thawed

2 teaspoons salt

1 1/4 teaspoons garam masala

1 tablespoon lemon juice

Cook potatoes in water for about 8 minutes, until soft.
Drain, mash, cover, and set aside.

In a sauté pan, heat olive oil, add coriander seeds, and
heat for about 15 seconds; they will turn dark brown. Add
onions, chilies, and ginger, and continue to cook 4 to 5
minutes. Add garam masala, salt, and lemon juice. In a bowl,
mix all filling ingredients.

PASTRY

4 tablespoons browned butter and 3 tablespoons vegetable
   oil, combined

1 package phyllo dough (10 sheets)

To prepare the pastries, heat oven to 400°F. Place 2 sheets of
phyllo dough on countertop, vertically. Lightly brush with
butter-oil mixture and cover with another sheet of phyllo.
Cut the phyllo in half, place about 1/2 cup of filling mixture
on each half of dough, and roll into a triangle. Continue
with remaining phyllo and filling to make 10 pastries.
   Bake at 400°F for 25 minutes, until golden brown.

VEGGIE BURGERS

2 tablespoons olive oil

5 ribs celery, minced

2 large onions, minced

3 large carrots, minced

2 heads garlic, minced

3 cups peanuts, roasted and coarsely chopped

3 cups sesame seeds, roasted and finely ground

3 cups sunflower seeds, roasted and coarsely chopped

2 cans navy beans, puréed separately

3 teaspoons mixed fresh or dried herbs (such as sage, basil,
   thyme)

Ancho chili powder

Black pepper, ground

8 cups cooked brown rice, blended until sticky; or 4 cups rice
   cooked in 7 cups water, blended until sticky

1/3 cup tamari

4 tablespoons tomato paste

2 tablespoons paprika

2 tablespoons fresh herbs, chopped

Salt to taste

6 to 8 eggs

1 to 2 cups matzo meal

Sauté minced vegetables in olive oil. Thoroughly mix
vegetables with remaining ingredients, except eggs and
matzo flour. Divide mixture into sixths or eighths, place into
plastic bags, and freeze.
   After thawing an individual bag of mixture, blend in
one beaten egg and 1/4 cup of matzo meal. Form mixture into
three 4-oz. patties. Grill or fry.

TROTTER'S CAFÉ AND BAKERY

Northwoods Organic Produce

Local, fresh, and flavorful pretty much describe the basics of Saint Paul's Trotter's Café, but if you add community involvement, sustainable practices in all they do, and philanthropy, you'll be closer to the total Trotter's concept.

For almost twenty years, Dick and Pat Trotter's plan has been to buy local. The Saint Paul Farmers' Market, Whole Farm Co-op, Peace Coffee, Nowak Dairy, and Northwoods Organic Produce are some of the producers who have provided the bulk of the food that goes into the soups, entrees, scones, bread, and cookies that are all made "from scratch" on a daily basis. Stocks are simmered, chickens are poached, and bread is proofed for a menu that changes weekly, always incorporating what's seasonal.

"In an urban environment, we feel it's very important to have a rural connection," Dick says. "By supporting local growers we can help them continue, and they help us to give our customers flavorful, fresh products. We feel good knowing who grows the food we use and where it comes from; we can put a name or a face with many of the ingredients we use."

One of those faces is Dave Massey's of Northwoods Organic Produce. Dave, who farms near Pequot Lakes, is a chemist who worked with glues and adhesives for three decades

Pat and Dick Trotter

before retiring from Saint Paul–based H. B. Fuller. Ultimately, he combined his skill for problem-solving with his longtime passion for organic gardening and now raises extraordinary vegetables, berries, and seeds.

Dave won't claim he spent his career thinking outside the box. "I was always on the outer margins of the box, though," he says. With that in mind, it's not surprising that everything he does on his farm diverges somewhat from the typical center-of-the-box organic farmer. Only a farmer-chemist-troubleshooter would precisely measure the sugar content in his squash.

"I have a Ukrainian squash variety that is the sweetest squash you can find," Dave claims. "I even had the sugar tested. Nobody else has that variety." Dave has multiplied his Ukrainian squash seeds, which he obtained years ago from the Seed Savers Exchange in Decorah, Iowa, to the point where he can grow it commercially. But even so, demand is so high he can't keep up.

Dick and Pat like working with producers like Dave who are passionate about what they do. And with the variety of products Dave and others provide, Dick and Pat can create many options for their diners. "We have many vegetarian dishes. I think the variety helps the customer venture out into trying something different, like checking out a new soup flavor and complementing it with a favorite bread. There's always a new combination to try," Pat says.

She adds, "Food brings people together. Our business has changed a lot over the years, and always for the better. We listen to our customers. You gauge your business by the 'regulars.'"

And the regulars know that if you tip for good service, good things will happen. The employees decided years ago to donate the majority of their tip money to local charities. Every week, Trotter's also donates food to a local food shelf and an area shelter. If you bring in your own to-go container, you'll save a tree *and* save five percent on your purchase. A different local artist's work can be seen on the walls each month. Community meetings are welcome at this neighborhood cafe.

Dick says, "We feel there are so many things you can do to make a difference." And they do.

Dave Massey

153

TRIPLE FRUIT SCONES

Makes 12 scones

3 cups organic white flour
$\frac{1}{3}$ cup sugar
1 tablespoon baking powder
$\frac{1}{2}$ teaspoon baking soda
$\frac{1}{4}$ teaspoon salt
3 oz. butter, cut into small pieces
$\frac{1}{3}$ cup chopped dried apricots
$\frac{1}{3}$ cup Craisins
1 egg
1 egg white
$\frac{3}{4}$ cup buttermilk
2 teaspoons orange rind

Combine flour, sugar, soda, baking powder, and salt in mixing bowl. Add the butter, apricots, and Craisins; mix until butter is in pea-size pieces.

In a separate bowl, combine egg and egg whites, buttermilk, and orange rind. Add this liquid to the dry ingredients and mix until it just comes together. Using your hands, knead several times in bowl and then place the dough on a lightly floured board. Form dough into a 12x6-inch rectangle. Cut into 12 triangular pieces. Bake on a cookie sheet at 350°F for 13 to 16 minutes, or until lightly browned.

CARROT DILL SOUP

This soup is best when made with early small and sweet carrots. Makes a delicious chilled summer soup too!

12 medium carrots, peeled and cut into 3-inch pieces
Half of a medium onion, diced small
$\frac{1}{2}$ cup unsalted butter
$\frac{1}{2}$ cup fresh dill, minced
1 to 2 cups 2% milk
Salt and pepper to taste

Sauté the onions and carrots in butter for 10 minutes. Add the fresh dill and cook for 5 more minutes. Cover carrots with water and simmer until carrots are tender. Process carrots and liquid until smooth (use either an immersion blender or purée in batches in an upright blender) and return to pan. Add milk until soup is the consistency of a cream soup. Season with salt and pepper.

ZESTY CORNBREAD

This is a wonderful moist cornbread that can be as zesty as you'd like to make it.

Makes one 9x9-inch loaf

2 eggs
1 cup buttermilk
¼ cup canola oil
⅓ cup honey
1 cup white flour
1 cup corn meal
1 tablespoon baking powder
½ teaspoon salt

Optional add-ins:
½ cup fresh or frozen corn
¼ cup fresh or canned green chilies
2 tablespoons chopped hydrated sun-dried tomatoes
½ cup shredded cheddar cheese

Preheat oven to 350°F. Grease a 9x9-inch square or 9-inch round pan.

Whisk together eggs, oil, honey, and buttermilk. Set aside. Combine flour, corn meal, baking powder, and salt. Blend together. Add wet ingredients to the dry mix. Stir to combine. Fold in optional ingredients.

Pour batter into greased pan and smooth the surface. Bake for 25 to 30 minutes. Serve with Minnesota syrup and butter, or honey butter.

SWEET POTATO OAT CURRANT BREAD

Makes 2 loaves

2 tablespoons yeast

1¼ cups warm water

1¼ cup puréed sweet potato (recipe below)

¼ cup molasses

½ tablespoon salt

1 cup oats, Minnesota organic

1 cup currants

4½ cups white flour, organic

1 cup whole wheat flour, organic

1 egg white

Dissolve yeast in 100 to 110°F warm water; allow to activate. Add sweet potatoes, molasses, and 1½ cups of white flour. Mix until smooth. Add salt, oats, and rest of flour. Knead for 5 minutes, then add currants, and knead for 7 minutes more.

Let rise until doubled, covered in a warm spot. Form into loaves (this dough is too soft for a free-form loaf; form into pan-size shaped loaves). Place into two 8x4½-inch greased loaf pans, cover, and let rise again until almost doubled in size. Brush the egg white on top of the loaves, sprinkle with oats, and bake at 350°F for 30 to 35 minutes.

PURÉED SWEET POTATOES

Make sure you put the sweet potatoes on a baking sheet; otherwise, they will ooze sweet, sticky juice all over your oven bottom.

Cut a small slit in 2 to 3 sweet potatoes and bake at 350°F until soft, 40 to 50 minutes. Cool to room temperature. Peel the sweet potatoes and process flesh in a food processor, fitted with a steel blade, until smooth.

ACKNOWLEDGEMENTS

Second Edition: This is version 1.5 of *The Minnesota Homegrown Cookbook*. What that means is that we updated a few stories where establishments have closed, moved, or where the principals have changed. Some of these restaurants and B&Bs may be working with additional farmers or different farmers. So in many ways, these stories are a snapshot in time, and we encourage you to visit the restaurants (or their websites) to see what is new.

In putting together version 1.5, much thanks goes to Elijah Goodwell, who led the effort and worked closely with Grace Brogan, who both coordinated updates and wrote new stories. Other thanks to photographers Mette Nielsen, Kris Hase, and Chad Johnson for providing excellent and timely photography. Our gratitude to Elizabeth Noll, Caitlin Fultz, and the good folks at Quarto Publishing, without whom this revision would not be possible.

—Jan Joannides, Renewing the Countryside, 2014

First Edition: *The Minnesota Homegrown Cookbook* has been a few years in the making. Even before the ink was dry on our first book, *Renewing the Countryside—Minnesota*, Tim King mentioned the idea of identifying small cafes and restaurants where you could get a good meal made from scratch. Always one to take up a good idea, Christy James, on her extensive travels throughout Minnesota, began sending us information on the great little cafes and restaurants she came across.

This book really got its wings when the North Central Sustainable Agriculture Research and Education (SARE) program provided a grant to Renewing the Countryside and its partners to boost awareness of sustainably grown foods. North Central SARE has done a world of good for local food systems through its support and promotion of sustainable farming and ranching.

Support from the W.K. Kellogg Foundation was also critical in bringing this project to life. Their support enables Renewing the Countryside to take on projects that help inform the public about important issues in our food system and in rural communities.

A knowledgeable and talented team of people contributed to the making of this book. The editorial committee, comprised of Mary Broeker, Tim King, Chuck Knierim, Brett Olson, Derric Pennington, Alice Tanghe, and myself, spent many hours concepting and creating the framework for this book.

Derric Pennington, Andi McDaniel, and Sarah Johnson did a great deal of research and preliminary interviews with cafes and restaurants. Their tenacious efforts laid the groundwork for this and other projects.

The stories were brought to life through the poetic writing of Tim King and Alice Tanghe. Tim—part poet, part activist, part farmer—fully understands the anticipation of receiving a seed catalogue mid-winter and the satisfaction of harvesting one's crops after a season of hard work. Alice is a "foodie" at heart with extensive experience in publishing. She is passionate about a good story and good food and knows all the great places to eat in the Twin Cities.

Tony Schreck's beautiful photos make up the illustrative backbone of this book. He traveled many miles to take the photos of the food, chefs, farmers, and landscapes you see here. Tony is renowned in the local media scene for being able to deliver amazing images from fast and painless location photo shoots.

The stunning stock photography of Richard Hamilton Smith, John Connell, and Kristi Link Fernholz helped us capture the "sense of place" of the different regions featured. As natives to those places, they have a unique ability to capture feeling in a photo. To tell the story of fishing on Lake Superior, John agreed to set out on a boat with Harley Tofte in October. While the pictures show a serene and placid lake, anyone who lives on the North Shore will tell you that October can bring white caps worthy of legend. And Kristi captured wonderful images from western Minnesota on unrealistic last-minute timelines.

Dave Holman came to Renewing the Countryside for a summer job straight out of college. He proved to be an accomplished photographer and shot several of the stories featured here. Sidney Brush, Robb Long, Karen Reed, Jodi Ohlsen Reed, Dave Hansen, and Alice Tanghe helped fill the gaps where we couldn't schedule photo shoots or the existing photos were too good to pass by.

This brings us to the food. While you'd think recipes from accomplished chefs wouldn't need to be tested, the reality is that most chefs don't work from recipes that most of us would understand. Most are artists and often work by feel . . . a little more salt here or five minutes longer there. So Alice Tanghe, Mary Broeker, and Brett Olson spent many hours deciphering, testing, and, when needed, adjusting recipes to serve a few people—rather than an entire restaurant. Many thanks to them for their time and talent and to the lucky people who sampled the dishes they prepared.

As editors, Alice Tanghe and Stephanie Larson whipped all the text for this book into shape. In addition to writing, recipe testing, and editing, Alice did the coordination for the Twin Cities portion of this book.

As creative director, Brett Olson developed much of the structure, look, and feel for the book. He also coordinated the photography and shot a number of the photos.

We are extremely grateful to Garrison Keillor for writing the foreword for this book.

A number of other people contributed to different aspects of this project, and we want to acknowledge and thank them. They include Margaret Schnieders, Lindsay Rehban, Beth Nelson, Helene Murray, JoAnne Berkenkamp, Colleen Tollefson, Mary Jo Forbord, Kent Gustafson, Paul Hugunin, Christy James, Marcia Neely, Terrance T. Nennich, Monica Siems, Courtney Tchida, Pam Thorsen, Cathy Twohig, Bill Wilcke, and Beth Munnich.

Thanks to the many folks across the state who sent in suggestions for restaurants, cafes, and bed and breakfasts to include in this book. We wish we could have included them all but had a limited amount of space. On our website you can find a link to a growing list of eateries that serve local food.

Lastly, a very special thanks to all the sustainable farmers across the state who are growing lovely and tasty food while caring for the environment and their communities and to all the chefs and cooks who incorporate these ingredients into their menus.

They are our local food heroes!

—Jan Joannides, Renewing the Countryside, 2008

Minnesota has an amazing array of government, nonprofit, and for-profit organizations working to strengthen and support the local food economy and bring great local foods to Minnesota. Find out more at www.renewingthecountryside.org.

RESTAURANT DIRECTORY

Alexis Bailly Vineyards
18200 Kirby Avenue South
Hastings, MN 55033
651.437.1413
www.abvwines.com

The Amboy Cottage Cafe
100 Maine Street East
Amboy, MN 56010
507.674.3123
www.amboycottagecafe.com

Angry Trout Cafe
P.O. Box 973
Grand Marais, MN 55604
218.387.1265
www.angrytroutcafe.com

Birchwood Cafe
3311 East 25th Street
Minneapolis, MN 55406
612.722.4474
www.birchwoodcafe.com

Brewed Awakenings Coffeehouse
24 Northeast 4th Street
Grand Rapids, MN 55744
218.327.0724
www.brewedawakenings.biz

Bryant Lake Bowl
810 West Lake Street
Minneapolis, MN 55408
612.825.3737
www.bryantlakebowl.com

Caribou Grill
225 East Broadway
Hallock, MN 56728
218.843.3740
www.caribougrill.net

Chez Jude
P.O. Box 277
Lutsen, Mn 55612
218-370-1335
www.chezjude.com

Corner Table
4257 Nicollet Avenue
Minneapolis, MN 55409
612.823.0011
www.cornertablerestaurant.com

Country Bed & Breakfast
17038 - 320th Street
Shafer, MN 55074
651.257.4773
www.countrybedandbreakfast.us

Dancing Winds Farm Stay
6863 County 12 Boulevard
Kenyon, MN 55946
507.789.6606

The Ellery House Bed and Breakfast
28 South 21st Avenue East
Duluth, MN 55812
800.355.3794
www.elleryhouse.com

El Norteno
Restaurant, Market and Deli
4000 East Lake Street
Minneapolis, MN 55406
612.722.6808

Gardens of Salonica
19 5th Street Northeast
Minneapolis, MN 55413
612.378.0611
www.gardensofsalonica.com

Heartland Restaurant & Farm Direct Market
289 East 5th Street
St. Paul, MN 55101
651-699-3536
www.heartlandrestaurant.com

Hell's Kitchen
80 South 9th St
Minneapolis, MN 55402
612.332.4700
www.HellsKitchenInc.com

Java River Cafe
210 South 1st Street
Montevideo, MN 56265
320.269.7106
www.javarivercafe.com

Lucia's Restaurant, Wine Bar, and To Go
1432 West 31st Street
Minneapolis, MN 55408
612.825.1572
www.lucias.com

Maplelag Resort
30501 Maplelag Road
Callaway, MN 56521
218.375.4466
www.maplelag.com

Mendoberri Cafe & Wine Bar
730 Main Street
Mendota Heights, MN 55118
651.209.3270
www.mendoberri.com

Minnesota Landscape Arboretum
3675 Arboretum Drive
Chaska, MN 55318
952.443.1422
www.arboretum.umn.edu

New Scenic Cafe
5461 North Shore Scenic Drive
Duluth, MN 55804
218.525.6274
www.sceniccafe.com

Nosh Restaurant & Bar
310-1/2 South Washington Street
Lake City, MN 55041
651.345.2425
www.noshrestaurant.com

The People's Food Co-op
519 1st Avenue Southwest
Rochester, MN 55902
507-289-9061
www.pfc.coop

Prairie Bay Restaurant
15115 Edgewood Drive
Baxter, MN 56425
218.824.6444
www.prairiebay.com

Restaurant Alma
528 University Avenue Southeast
Minneapolis, MN 55414
612.379.4909
www.restaurantalma.com

Scandinavian Inn
701 Kenilworth Avenue South
Lanesboro, MN 55949
507.467.4500
www.scandinavianinn.com

Spoonriver Restaurant
750 South 2nd Street
Minneapolis, MN 55401
www.spoonriver.com
612.436.2236

St. Peter Food Co-op
119 West Broadway
St. Peter, MN 56082
507.934.4880
www.stpeterfood.coop

Trotter's Cafe
232 North Cleveland Avenue
St. Paul, MN 55104
651.645.8950
www.trotters-stpaul.com

Waves of Superior Cafe
20 Surfside Drive
Tofte, MN 55615
218-663-6877
www.surfsideonsuperior.com

Wild Hare Bistro
523 Minnesota Avenue Northwest
Bemidji, MN 56601
218.444.5282
www.wildharebistro.com

Writing Credits:
Stories written by Tim King: Angry Trout Cafe—Dockside Fish Market; Ellery House Bed and Breakfast—Park Lake Farm; New Scenic Cafe—Bay Produce; The Amboy Cottage Cafe—Whole Grain Milling Company; Java River Cafe—Dry Weather Creek Farm; Saint Peter Food Co-op—Shepherd's Way Farms; Caribou Grill—Double J Elk; Nosh Restaurant & Bar—Rochester Farmers Market; Scandinavian Inn—Hilltop Acres Farm; Dancing Winds Farmstay Retreat—Callister Farm; Brewed Awakenings Coffeehouse—Spica Farm; Country Bed & Breakfast—Steve Anderson Sugarbush

Stories written by Alice Tanghe: Restaurant Alma—Otter Creek Growers; Bryant Lake Bowl—Moonstone Farm; Birchwood Cafe—Riverbend Farm; El Norteño—Whole Farm Co-op; Gardens of Salonica—Hill and Vale Farm; Heartland—Cedar Summit; Hell's Kitchen—Silver Bison Ranch; Lucia's—Fischer Farm; Minnesota Landscape Arboretum and Good Life Catering; Spoonriver—Mill City Farmers' Market; Trotters Café and Bakery—Northwoods Organic Produce

Stories written by Elijah Goodwell: Chez Jude—DragSmith Farms; Maplelag Resort—Hope Creamery; People's Food Co-op—DreamAcres*; Mendoberri Café & Wine Bar—Thousand Hills Cattle Company*; Alexis Bailly Vineyards—Northern Lights Blue*
*with Tim King

Stories written by Grace Brogan: Wild Hare Bistro—Farmucopia; Corner Table—Stone's Throw Urban Farm

Stories written by Tim King and Arlene Jones: Prairie Bay—The Farm on St. Mathias

Photo Credits:
Alexis Bailly Vineyard, 143; Bluefin Bay Resort, 23; Sidney Brush, 97; Katie Cannon, 122 top; John Connelly, 11, 15 right, 34, 35; DragSmith Farms, 19; The Farm on St. Mathias, 36, 37; Kristi Link Fernholz, 74, 75 right, 76, 77 bottom; E. J. Goodman, 145; David Hansen, 17; Kris Hase, 30, 31, 112, 114–115; David Holman, 22 top bottom, 44, 75 left, 149 top; Chad Johnson, 96; Lara Leimbach, 18; Robb Long, 80 bottom; Marina Lovell, 57, 59; Mette Nielsen, 22 top-left, top-right, and bottom; Brett Olson, 1, 2 top-right, 5 left, 6 left, 7 right and left, 8, 9, 10, 22 middle, 39 top left, 52, 53, 54, 59, 61, 63, 66–67, 69, 70 bottom right, 72, 77 top, 81, 82–83, 85 left, 91, 101 top-left and right, 104, 105, 109, 124 bottom, 126, 127, 128, 132, 133, 135 top, 149 bottom; Jodi Ohlsen Reed, 79 right, 80 top right; Karen Reed, 80 top right; Jay Richards, 62, 65; Moni Schneider, 56, 58, 60; Anthony Brett Schreck, 2 top-left and bottom left and right, 6 right, 14, 15 left, 16, 24, 25, 27, 29, 32, 33, 39 bottom, 40, 41, 42, 43 right, 46, 47, 49, 50–51, 68, 70, 71, 73, 78, 79 left, 84, 86, 87, 89, 90, 92, 93, 100, 101 bottom left and right, 103, 106, 107, 110, 111, 112, 113, 115, 116, 119, 121, 124 top, 125, 130, 134, 135 bottom, 138, 148, 151, 152, 153; Alex Steinberg, 123; Brad Smith, 99; Richard Hamilton Smith, 12, 13; Larry Sobaskie, 142; Alice Tanghe, 146; Stone's Throw Urban Farm, 122 bottom; Tom Thulen, 20.

INDEX

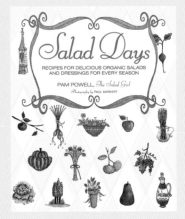

Salad Days
9780760340431

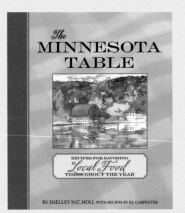

The Minnesota Table
9780760347683

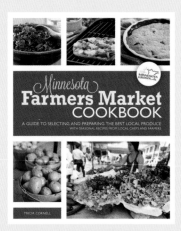

**The Minnesota
Farmers Market**
9780760344866

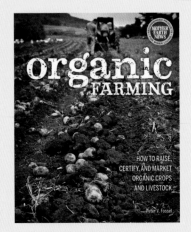

Organic Farming
9780760345719

**Landscaping with Native
Plants of Minnesota,
2nd edition**
9780760341186

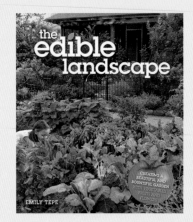

The Edible Landscape
9780760341391